THINK BIG!

THINK BIG!

*Be Positive and Be Brave
to Achieve Your Dreams*

RYUHO OKAWA

IRH Press

IRH PRESS
New York

Library of Congress Cataloging-in-Publication Data

ISBN 13: 978-1-942125-04-4
ISBN 10: 1942125046

Printed in China
First edition
Third printing

Cover Designer: Karla Baker

Contents

PREFACE

Those of you in the younger generations are probably facing many obstacles that seem to you like overwhelming adversity. Many of you are probably troubled by inferiority complexes. On the other hand, overconfidence has probably also vexed the majority of us.

If these words describe you, I hope that you will see that it is one of the perks of youth to face the challenge of building the path to our future, even as our minds keep swaying back and forth between our feelings of inferiority and overconfidence.

My gift to you is this message: Think big! No matter how high the Tokyo Sky Tree towers above the capital, it can never grow taller than its original design. So always dream big in your heart, and work persistently, step by step, to make your dreams come true. And when the moment of truth arrives in your life, be brave. Be determined to build the future of your dreams.

Ryuho Okawa
Founder and CEO
Happy Science Group
February 14, 2012

BUILDING
A BRIGHT FUTURE

· 1 ·

MY EXPERIENCES USING ENGLISH IN THE UNITED STATES

●————————————————————————●

My Struggle With the Question "Pardon?"

This chapter is dedicated to the younger generations who are in school or who have recently become members of working society. I would like to share some of the valuable principles I have learned that can help people in all kinds of circumstances lead successful lives and build a bright future.

When I think back to my younger years, I am reminded of the tough times I had in New York City, where I used to work for a general trading company. I was faced with the difficulties of working in a foreign country, and I had my share of struggles with the English language. I was only in my second year with the company when they decided to relocate me from Japan to New York City. Upon my arrival, I was given only five days for a briefing from the colleague whose responsibilities I was assigned to take over. Unfortunately, I was also suffering from the worst jet lag, as this was the first time I had ever gone abroad. With day and night completely reversed, it was impossible to think straight for almost a week. I remember that the briefings felt as if the words came from a distant place. I could hardly comprehend them, even though everything was being explained to me in Japanese.

Soon enough, my predecessor disappeared, and I was still so spaced out that I could hardly make out the meaning of my own native language. He left for a vacation on the West Coast, from where he would head straight for Japan. So there I was, left with a big desk and chair, a phone, an IBM typewriter, and the Apple II computer created by the famous Steve Jobs. The Apple II was not yet being sold on a full scale in the Japanese market, but it was very popular in the United States, as Americans were already using personal computers by this time.

Still in a groggy state from jet lag, I was at my desk, receiving countless phone calls every day. The phone rang anywhere from 100 to 150 times per day. Even worse, all the calls were, of course, in English. The office became a place of terror for me. When I think of those days, I am reminded of the horrible memory of one loathsome word: "Pardon?" Callers would often say to me, "Pardon?" or "I beg your pardon?" In short, they had such a difficult time understanding my English that they were asking me to repeat myself. Being asked three times was enough to make me feel completely discouraged about my English skills; my English was obviously unintelligible to a native speaker.

"Pardon?" was not the only word that disheartened me. I also struggled with being asked, "Is there anyone who can speak English?" Obviously, they were requesting to speak with someone else who could speak English better than I could. But when I looked around, all Japanese colleagues who spoke fluent English were engaged in other calls, and all the American employees were equally busy taking their own calls. There was never anyone who could help me. As you can imagine, the first week or so at the new office was filled with a sense of frustration with myself.

Saying "I Can" Was My Turning Point

As soon as I heard callers say, "Is there anyone..." they didn't have to finish their sentence for me to know what they were going to ask. But, of course, there was no one else I could ask to take the call for me. So I gathered my courage. I spoke into the receiver in a deliberately low and deep voice and said, "I can!" My callers hesitated and paused for a moment out of fear that they may have offended me. This was my chance. I used this pause to my full advantage; as soon as they flinched and paused, I belted out all the words that came to mind.

I knew that if I gave them more than two seconds, they

would throw the word "pardon" at me. I also knew that if I got three "pardons," it would be over for the little confidence I had left, so I made up my mind not to give them that opportunity. I answered, "I can!" and quickly fired into the receiver all the English I could think of. Even if they had difficulty understanding what I wanted to say in the beginning, once I had enough time to say more words, they eventually responded, "OK, I understand." By telling them as many words as I could that described the context of what I wanted to convey, I was gradually starting to get through to people.

This marked my turning point. I completely changed my attitude, and I made up my mind to never again give anyone the chance to say, "Pardon?" to me. It was too humiliating to be asked whether I could switch places with someone who could speak better English. So I made the resolution to say, "I can," and explain that there was no one else who could take their call.

In the beginning, there were times when I asked other people to take my calls. But I realized that I would be giving in to defeat if I continued to do that, so I resolved to stop passing on my calls to anyone. This complete change in my attitude, at the age of twenty-five or twenty-six, was a turning point. Of course, it was extremely difficult for me to confidently say, without any inward hesitation, that I could speak English, when I knew full well that my English skills were lacking. After all, I then had to come up with actual things to say in English! But having the courage to respond to my callers with this boldness marked a valuable beginning for me.

I had not studied English as much as I should have before leaving for the United States, because I thought that I would automatically learn it once I was there. I had completely underestimated how difficult it was going to be. As a result of my ignorance, I went through a tough time but being forced to work on my skills taught me many things. Many people probably thought that I had a lot of nerve going to the United States with my level of English, but the truth was simply that I had no idea how difficult it was going to be.

I Realized that Wall Street Was a Battlefield for the Best of the Best

It was in 1982 that I was handed a letter of appointment, from a forty-seven-year-old manager of the foreign exchange department, transferring me to the company's office in the United States. I was twenty-five or twenty-six at the time, and my monthly salary was approximately the equivalent of $5,500. When the manager handed me the letter of appointment, he made a point of telling me that my salary would now be the same as his own. So it happened that I was sent to the United States with a salary equal to a manager of the foreign exchange department. Though I had not realized it at the time, this was his way of telling me how tough a job it was to work on Wall Street.

It had not completely dawned on me at the time that the best of the best from all over the world, as well as all over America, were sent to Wall Street, the site of the New York Stock Exchange in lower Manhattan. My company had decided to send me there to compete with these top American businesspeople, but I was not yet fully aware of the magnitude of the expectations set upon me. As a result, my new colleagues were appalled that someone like me, who had difficulty speaking English fluently, had been sent there. The first week was a tirade of criticism, and with this initiation into the tough world of Wall Street, I began my career practically groveling.

In this chapter, I would like to share with the younger generations some of my memories of this time in my life and point out the lessons I learned about how we should think and what we can do to create a positive future for ourselves.

· 2 ·

HAVE A DREAM
AND PERSIST UNTIL IT COMES TRUE

●────────────────────────────●

Set a Big Goal and Create Interim Goals

Have a dream! This is my message to all members of younger generations who have a long future ahead of them. This is a big topic for everyone. You cannot possibly create a bright future for yourself without a dream to pursue. Know exactly what you want to achieve and make sure to dream big! It is in the very fabric of our nature as human beings to chase our dreams. And if you don't have a dream, you should take it as a valuable sign that you are not yet thinking of your future. If you find yourself without ideals, find your dream and start building your future.

The next step is to start making an effort to make your dream come true. You need to have a dream in the first place, but you also need to make sure that you work on making it a reality. This may sound like a matter of fact, but it is not an easy thing to do. Don't be just a dreamer waiting for the dream to come to you. Whether your dreams come true depends on how much effort and perseverance you put into them. I do not want anyone to end their lives only dreaming about their ideals. So keep asking yourself, "What can I do to make this dream come true?" And once you start working toward your dreams, you will have already started blazing a path to your future.

When you start working on your dreams, you first need to have a clear idea of your goals. You can start by setting yourself a big goal. Then, you should set yourself smaller and middle-term goals to aim for on the way. For example, many students have goals like, "After I graduate, I want to achieve this and that within three years," or "I want to do this and that before I am thirty." If you are around thirty years old, then you might want to think about what you will achieve by the age of forty. As you decide on larger goals like these, you will also want to think about the things you want to achieve on the way to these larger goals.

Develop a Wide Range of Interests in Your College Years

Many college students have too many dreams to be able to decide what they want to pursue. If this is true for you, there is no need to fret. What is most important is to experiment with a variety of things during your college years. Use this stage in your life to study a certain subject, experience something new, develop hobbies, spend time with friends who share your interests, and expand your interests into new areas. Get involved in anything that interests you, because this can lead to great opportunities and new beginnings later on in life, in your middle or senior years. Of course, some people will continue expanding into new areas even after they start working. But I recommend that students pursue their hobbies and interests while they are still in college, because these are the activities that most often flower into something later in life. So I encourage you all to expand your horizons as far as possible. Make an effort to develop a variety of interests and passions as you keep a look out for new possibilities within yourself. Not every interest will be immediately useful to your career, but as long as you feel passionate about something and have some experience with it, it will flower in unexpected ways and serve you well. Our college years are a very precious stage of our lives.

The Books We Read In Depth in Our Younger Years Have a Lasting Influence

I have found that the books we read in college leave a deep impression on us and remain fresh in our memories throughout life. Interestingly, regardless of the large number of books I've read since my graduation, the ones that I remember best over the decades of my life are those I read as a college student. You will find that those works that especially fascinated you and that you devoured as a student will influence the important choices you make in life.

Especially in our thirties and early forties, all of us are faced with major life decisions. Everyone assumes that we are basing our decisions on our own unique ideas, but in many cases, this is not entirely true. When you think back, you will notice that your decisions are based on the philosophies of thinkers and authors whose ideas strongly resonated with you between, say, the age of twenty and twenty-two. The books we love at that stage of our lives and read repeatedly become a very deep part of us and have a tremendous impact on our way of thinking. This impact lasts through many decades. When you read and internalize books this way, you begin to develop your own philosophy. Soon enough, you may find that your ideas have become independent of those of your parents, and your and your parents' aims will grow apart. This process is the beginning of your philosophical emancipation.

Avoid Books By Authors
with Destructive Characteristics

If the kinds of books and philosophies that you encounter when you are young have a destructive quality and you become absorbed in them, it can have a disastrous effect on your life. Whether we encounter ideas that have positive or negative effects might depend on our luck. If we encounter ideologies that have a negative impact on us, we can end up making the wrong decisions, and life can become a tragedy. So we should not believe that all writers should be held in high regard. Pay careful attention to the characteristics of their works as a whole and the writer's way of life, all the way through to death. Ask yourself whether you would like to have the same kind of life. It is particularly important to stay away from writers who led destructive lives, because if you read too many of their works, their ideas can influence your way of thinking.

For example, authors who died by suicide might have had very pure personalities. We might feel compelled to sympathize with them. However, if, by reading their works over and over, your perspective becomes too associated with their thought patterns, you could begin making the same kind of judgments and develop a similar tendency to seek tragedy. Many novelists who write about their hardships might write stories about poverty, bankruptcy, illnesses, and failed relationships, and these stories make their works interesting. If you admire these authors too much, though, chances are that you will start to emulate their lives. If I admire a novelist who romanticizes poverty, for example, I might begin seeking poverty for myself. Even if you consciously say that you want a higher salary, this romanticization of poverty will take root in your subconscious, and a desire for bankruptcy and failure in your business may creep up on you.

Our Philosophies Have Tremendous Influence over Our Lives

The philosophies that we believe in exercise tremendous influence over our lives. If the ideas we indulge in influence us only to a superficial extent, they will eventually disappear. But when they penetrate the surface and take root in our subconscious, they have a huge impact on our lives and the course of our future.

Philosophies are like rain. Sometimes, the rain just wets the surface of the soil. Other times, it rains enough to penetrate deep into the groundwater. Once the rain mixes with our groundwater—the ideas running through our subconscious—it starts to influence our lives. This is why it is very important to be aware of the ideas that penetrate the surface and become a powerful force in the depths of our lives. The books you read repeatedly, the things you think about constantly, and the things that you are always trying to learn all become part of your own philosophy.

Even if it is someone else's work that you read, if that

work strongly resonates with you, it means that you will start to grow similar to that author. It does not matter if these ideas came from someone else, because the fact that their philosophies resonated with you means that you already hold the same philosophy or that you have started to form similar ideas. Therefore, it is someone else's philosophy, but it is also your own philosophy. They were someone else's ideas in the beginning, but if you felt a strong interest in them and read them over and over, so much that they have become a part of you, then they have become your own philosophy that you will base your decisions on throughout life.

The Seeds We Sow in Our Minds Determine Our Future

Our philosophies are like seeds. The types of flowers that will blossom and the kind of fruits that will grow depend on the seeds you sow. Our philosophies have tremendous power to create something concrete and real; they are not just abstract concepts. Since our philosophy becomes actualized over time, you can tell what kind of person you are by checking your philosophy.

For example, one day, I conceived the idea of building a middle school and high school near Nasu Shoja in Tochigi Prefecture, where we own some land. A few years later, the Happy Science Academy was built, and my vision of building a school became a reality. If I had never thought of building a school, we would have never built one. If we kept thinking that schools need to be easily accessible by train, Happy Science Academy would have never been created. But since I had the idea of building a boarding school that would not require a commute by train, we were able to build one near Nasu Shoja, which is located in the countryside.

This is how powerful ideas are. Once you sow the seed, it begins to grow into a real plant. So always remember that you need to have the idea first, and then it will become actualized into reality. Be careful of what seeds you sow in your mind, because they will determine the melody of your life as they grow into the song of your future.

· 3 ·
THINK POSITIVE

Don't Let Negative Thinking Take Root in Your Mind

In our younger years, we are susceptible to sad, tragic, and unhappy events. We tend to be emotionally vulnerable and very sensitive during this stage of our lives. For example, personal events such as a relative's death, accident, or illness can easily influence and grip a younger person's supple mind. We should not let such events keep hold of us for too long, because a strong reaction to them can develop into a desire for unhappiness, sometimes to the point that we feel uncomfortable, as if we are not ourselves, without this state of misery. Our minds are very emotionally susceptible during our younger years, and this makes it all the more important that we never allow negative thoughts, ideas, and philosophies to take root in our minds.

"I failed once, so I must be a complete failure."
"I've been criticized. I don't think I can keep doing this anymore."

"I was told that I am useless at my job. I'm a hopeless failure."

"I was told that I am a bad student. There is no future for me."

"There is no hope for me, because I didn't get into a good school."

"My parents hate me, so there is no hope for me."

"My friend ignored me. She probably doesn't want to be friends anymore."

"My life is over because I failed in my business."

You probably have a lot of negative thoughts like the ones listed above. But do not let them take root in your mind.

Believe Strongly that You Will Grow Like Bamboo

It is a great fact that we can never think two different thoughts at the same time. If you find that a negative thought has come into your mind, just replace it with a positive one. Whenever you see or think negatively, think about an alternative, positive way of looking at the situation or problem at hand.

Even when you are faced with the most difficult trials of your life, you can always change your way of perceiving these situations. All you have to do is look at it from the opposite angle. For example, think to yourself, "This is a tough situation I'm in, but if I think about it, maybe something positive could come out of it," or, "He has been criticizing me very harshly, but what he is saying is not actually wrong. Perhaps this is my chance to overcome and grow from my weaknesses. Maybe he is actually trying to teach me something that is important to me." No matter how challenging the problems are that you encounter through life, you can change the way you perceive them and choose to face them with a positive and constructive attitude. The seeds of positivity and constructiveness that you germinate will assuredly blossom and ripen into a positive and constructive future.

On our journey through growth, we often face resistance. People around you may criticize you or try to bring you down. Sometimes you might find yourself being held back by the love of your well-meaning parents or by the envy of your teachers and professors at school or colleagues and superiors at work. In times like these, think about the strength and resilience of bamboo shoots. They are so strong that they will sprout anywhere, even through the floor. You can be strong and keep growing like a bamboo shoot. If you keep thinking strongly about reaching higher and growing taller, no matter what you are faced with, you will assuredly create a bright future.

It is also valuable to have resilience in times like these. The emotional vulnerability of our younger years makes us susceptible to hurt and unhappy feelings. There will be times when you feel hurt, feel down from being criticized or ridiculed, or feel like a failure because of a setback; you may feel so disappointed that you cannot imagine yourself ever becoming anyone extraordinary. Put a stop to these thoughts. Be strong, and get back up. Find the strength to pull yourself back up when you fall down. When you wake up the next morning, get up even stronger and with greater energy than the day before. No matter how many times you are knocked down, never give up, and keep getting back up on your feet.

· 4 ·

FAITH IS THE GREATEST WEAPON AGAINST FEAR

There Is Nothing to Fear, For We Are One with God

The foremost adversary that we have to fight when we are young is fear. All of us hold many fears, and most of them originate in a fear of the unknown. When the movie Jaws came out, the thought of a shark made us afraid to take a swim in the surf. Even if you were guaranteed that there were no sharks that day, just the thought of one might have glued your feet to the safety of the sandy beaches. This happens because the thought of encountering our fear can paralyze us into a state of terror. This is when we need courage.

What can we do to overcome our fears? Use the most powerful weapon against fear: faith. Conquer your fears through your faith in God. Believe very strongly that if we are one with God, there is nothing to be afraid of. We all have the ability to build a bright future. Give yourself encouragement by saying that you are a disciple and a child of God, that you believe in Him, and since He is always with you, you should fear nothing. If we have been following the Truths, this is even more reason for us to fear nothing, for our future cannot be unhappy and our fears can never defeat us as long as we are one with God. It is my hope that you will fight your fears with faith.

Make Effort Upon Effort — Keep Persevering

Use the power of belief to keep fighting your fears, and as you think about your dreams, make real efforts to make them come true. I have found one common denominator in everyone who has achieved success, and this common denominator is unrelenting persistence. All successful people have made effort upon effort and have kept persevering in pursuit of their dreams. It is not about making an effort just once. Success is found in never giving up—in persevering toward your dreams, one step at a time. There are no exceptions to this law of success. Luck may bring you one-time successes like winning the lottery or winning a bet, but this kind of success is fleeting.

To become successful, first make sure that you have a dream. Then, conquer your fears through faith. And finally, never stop persevering and make a constant effort toward actualizing your dreams into reality. This mindset of constant effort and devotion is about giving it extra effort even after you have given it all you've got. Where someone else would have stopped and given up, you will think, "I'm going to keep going and take another step."

· 5 ·

HOW TO USE THE TWENTY-FOUR HOURS OF YOUR DAY

Using Small Chunks of Time Will Lead You to Success

Everyone is equally given twenty-four hours each day, and how we use these hours determines our future. The number of years everyone lives varies, but everyone is given the same exact length of time each day, no matter who you are.

So, how should we use our twenty-four hours to find success? There are two things I strongly recommend. One of them is to treasure every little chunk of time—every minute and every second. If you can find fifteen minutes or even just ten minutes in your day, put them to use! It will not get you anywhere to keep putting things off and believing that you will study when you have a larger block of time. There is nothing wrong with scheduling leisure activities for a later time—for example, during summer break or the holidays—but procrastination will never help you in your studies.

I have found that successful people have the habit of

looking for any short fragments of time they can find, even if it is just ten or fifteen minutes—and using that time to study. If you want to learn a new language, for example, you need to make use of every minute you can find. All experts in any foreign language use these small chunks of time throughout the day—on the train, during their lunch break at work, in the bath, and before they go to bed. All these little chunks of time can be used productively, and it is very difficult to become an expert at a language unless you do this. There is no such thing as a linguistic genius who never made this kind of effort.

All of us, no matter who we are, have no more and no less than twenty-four hours a day, including our sleeping time. So the high road to our dreams lies in using every minute of the day efficiently and being persistent in our efforts. This is something that also applies to adults. Once we begin working full time, it becomes increasingly difficult to find large chunks of time. We can barely ever find two hours or even one hour in our day, so every little bit of time is precious.

Develop a Brain
that Is Both Masculine and Feminine

The second thing that I strongly suggest is to create a habit of multitasking. You will need to do many things simulta-

Chapter ① **BUILDING A BRIGHT FUTURE**

neously to get things done. In general, the male brain has a propensity for intense, long-term effort. For example, the pyramids in Egypt were built with this sort of a male mentality. The Egyptians concentrated on completing one pyramid at a time before they moved on to the next one. They finished building the Sphinx before beginning their next pyramid. This is how the masculine brain tends to work on one thing over a long period of time.

Highly educated women, especially those who compete with men on a daily basis, usually also develop a strong masculine brain. The masculine brain is essential for highly specialized jobs that require focusing on one thing for a long time, but it will only help you become a moderately capable person. The masculine way of working is a basic ability that all jobs require, but it will not take you beyond that basic level.

In contrast to the male brain, the female brain can do many things at once. Women are thought to be born with multitasking skills. Historically, women have been responsible for managing the household and raising many children at once. With three, four, or five children running around, causing trouble, falling, crying, and laughing, all while that dinner is cooking on the stove, women have had to multitask. To be women, their senses have always had to be on high alert; they had to be aware of everything that is happening around them so they can focus on many things at once. That is why many women are great multitaskers. Some highly educated women, especially women who are strong in math and science, may develop a stronger masculine brain than a feminine brain. But most women are naturally born with the ability to multitask and retain this ability throughout their lives. In everyday life and for practical issues, multitasking is not the most difficult skill to develop. The challenge is in developing multitasking skills at work. If you are young and want to create a bright future for yourself, it is important to develop both of these skills from the masculine and feminine brains, as you also work with your strengths.

Keep Your Eyes On Multiple Things As You Multitask

It is important to try to find a balance between your masculine and your feminine brain. On one hand, you want a masculine brain that focuses on one task at a time and executes it to completion; on the other hand, you also want a feminine brain that can watch multiple things simultaneously from a wider angle, like the dragonfly that possesses many eyes. Develop the ability to see everything that is happening as if you had many eyes. Run many tasks at once.

To do this, you can start all your tasks at once and work on them at the same speed, or you can start them at different stages or work on them at different speeds. It's fine to have one project that is almost at the stage of completion, a second one that is half-finished, and a third one that has just been started. The key is to have various jobs running at the same time to ensure that you will be able to accomplish many things. Making a conscious effort to balance the masculine brain with the feminine will help you get many things done simultaneously.

This reminds me of fighter-plane pilots, who need to be capable of parallel processing. Fighter planes engaging in battle face enemies from all directions: the front, the back, the sides, above, and below. Interestingly, people who excel too much at concentrating on one point do not make good fighter-plane pilots. It only takes one shot to shoot down someone who can only see what is in front of them. To fly fighter planes, your personality needs to shift focus frequently enough to be able to react to shots that can come from anywhere. Fighter-plane pilots are also expected to make comprehensive judgments, which make them not just soldiers, but also candidates for high-level positions.

In a large city, many trains and subways run on multiple tracks simultaneously. Similarly, in the final analysis, we can say that to be successful at what you do, you need to try your best to learn multitasking and master parallel processing.

If Multitasking Is Difficult,
Then Make Decisions Quickly

If multiple processing is difficult for you, you can create waves of work by focusing on one important thing and then shifting your concentration onto the next thing. Another method you can try is to make decisions quickly, take action immediately, and finish each task speedily. Do not postpone today's work to tomorrow. If you get it done today, you will have time to tackle the next task tomorrow, and in the end, you will achieve the same results that you would have if you had been working on several jobs simultaneously. In short, it is essential that we not procrastinate things.

In my case, I hardly ever postpone any of my tasks. I make decisions immediately and make sure that everything I need to do gets done quickly. As a result, my desk is always clear of work. Since all my tasks are taken care of immediately, my hands are always free, and my mind is always at ease. You can easily keep procrastinating and postponing your work, but I prefer to take care of things immediately and wrap them up on the spot, because if you hold on to a task, you will be in trouble when a new task comes to you. If that is followed by another task, your task list can become very long, and then you have to think of a way to finish everything at once. This is why, when I am given work, I look at it and make a decision right away. Even if I make the wrong decision, all I have to do is fix it later. Frequent revisions are an inevitable part of life, so accept that and change your approach: make decisions right on the spot, and revise them later if any of them were wrong. Otherwise, it will be impossible for you to get more things done.

Create a Golden Future

So far, I have shared with you many suggestions on how to use your twenty-four hours to the fullest to achieve success. Let me sum things up. First, find small chunks of time and use them. Next, develop the ability to multitask and to handle multiple things that pop up. Finally, if multitasking is not your style, then learn to make decisions immediately and wrap things up quickly so that you are never holding on to jobs. Finish every task that comes to you as quickly as possible so that your desk is always clear of work and you are ready to take on new tasks at any time.

As long as you follow this advice, you will be promoted—no matter what department or position you are currently in. Since there are few people who can master these skills, you will be respected as a very capable employee and for always being at ease with the amount of work you have. Your promotions will stop when you start working at the top limit of your abilities. So you have to always appear as if you are confident and at ease with the work you are being given. If, in fact, you really are at ease with the skills that your current position requires from you, then you will continue to be promoted until you reach your limit. Your future is sure to be golden!

I hope that younger readers have learned what they should do to begin their road to success and create a bright future for themselves. I have scattered many seeds for success throughout this chapter. In fact, these seeds are also valuable advice for those who want to become part of the elite. Everything I have said can be applied to many situations in life. So even if you cannot fully understand all my suggestions right away, take your time, and think about how you can apply them to yourself right now.

Please believe that you have a bright future ahead of you. Have faith, and live a positive, constructive life. What matters is being positive and productive. Do not think negatively. Think positive. Keep looking forward, and the path will open up for you. This is a recipe not only for individual success, but also for a new, brighter future for our entire civilization.

2

AIM TO ACHIEVE SUCCESS GRACEFULLY!

· 1 ·

THE "I'M FINE!" SPIRIT

A High School Memory

In this chapter I would like to discuss some themes from my book called *"I'm Fine" Spirit*. The phrase "I'm fine" reminds me of a fond memory of my high school English Composition class. This class was held on Monday mornings, which was the worst time of the week because our minds were not yet alert. Back then, conversational exercises were incorporated into our English composition classes, probably because conversation classes did not yet exist. My English teacher had a special policy: he always kicked off our weeks with a burst of energy. So every Monday morning, he would start our week by getting up at the podium and engaging us in conversation in English. He would pick a student and ask, "How are you?"

I used to sit in the front row, so naturally, I was one of the students who was chosen. One day, he pointed to me and asked, "How are you?" I replied honestly, "I'm not so good" or "I'm tired." Then he said to me that the polite thing to say is, "I'm fine, thank you. And you?" But—honest student that I was—I was not convinced. So I asked him, "But what if I had a cold? Wouldn't I be lying if I said that I was doing fine?" My teacher responded by saying that we should still say, "I'm fine," and then follow it by saying that we are a little bit under the weather. He taught us that we should never say something like, "I'm not feeling so well," or "I'm really tired today," or, "It's a blue Monday." It was very important to him that we always replied, "I'm fine!"

To this day, I still remember this conversation with my high school English teacher. By now, my recollection of much else from his class has faded. But since then, I have often remembered what he taught me that day because I felt the truth in his words. He was right. We should never start our week with negative remarks such as, "I'm tired" or "I don't feel well." No matter how exhausted you may actually feel, your first words should be "I'm fine!" You can always talk about how you are tired after that. This is an important way of being polite to the person you are talking to—and it is also a positive way of disciplining yourself. That day, I learned how positive the English language is.

A Japanese Prime Minister's Accidental Zen Koan

There is an interesting story about a conversation that a Japanese prime minister had with former United States President Bill Clinton during his visit to Japan. When President Clinton arrived, the Japanese prime minister went to welcome him and shake his hand. But when he tried to say, "How are you?" he accidentally asked, "Who are you?"

If he had been asked, "How are you?" I am sure that President Clinton would have responded with "I'm fine!" or something along those lines. However, since he was asked, "Who are you?" he responded, "I'm Mrs. Clinton's husband." Indeed, it was a classy response.

This story could have been only a rumor. Since very few people could have witnessed this scene, we may never know whether it actually happened. But considering that it was the same prime minister who pronounced the pronoun "it" when he was trying to read the acronym "IT," it would not be surprising if it were a true story. For us Japanese, phrases such as "How are you?" "Who are you?" and "How do you do?" are hard to understand, and the words get stuck in our throats when we try to use them in real life.

But I will not drag our former prime minister through the dirt too much. Maybe there was a deeper meaning behind his question, like the deep meaning behind a Zen koan. I am sure that most people would have had to pause and think about how to answer that question. If someone had asked me "Who are you?" I would have paused and wondered, "Should I say that I am El Cantare? Or should I give a different kind of answer?" From the exchange between Bill Clinton and the Japanese prime minister, we can see that greetings are very important.

Our Attitude Makes Us Who We Are

We should always be mindful of what we say, because our words build our perception of life. I mention this many times throughout this book, as well as in many talks, because I can never say this enough: what is most important in our lives is what we are always thinking about. A thought that you had on any given day is not going to have a significant effect on your life. On the other hand, the ideas that you have been thinking about all the time over the course of a year, three years, five years, ten years, or twenty years are the ideas that build who you are. The attitude of your mind is what is important. This is not just an old saying. It is true. It is real. The thoughts that repeat themselves in your mind may not be visible to the eye, but they create your future. This is something that I mention at every opportunity, because I would like as many people as possible to experience this truth.

The "I'm fine!" spirit is a mindset that I hope everyone will adopt. I once said in a lecture called "Never Lose Your Hungry Spirit,"* that you will never grow old, no matter

---

* See Ryuho Okawa, *The Laws of Courage* (Tokyo: IRH Press, 2009). The lecture was held on October 6, 2007, at Tokyo Shoshinkan, Happy Science.

how old you may be, as long as you never stop thirsting for new knowledge and further self-improvement. I believe that the "I'm fine!" mentality is as valuable for people in the older generations as it is for younger people. To keep having the strength to smile and say "I'm fine!" when you are ill from old age, bedridden at the hospital, or being cared for at home is a positive way of living our lives and a way of giving people love, too. So from now on, whenever you feel so down that a negative thought is about to slip from your lips, adopt a positive attitude and say instead, "I'm feeling great! I'm doing really well!"

· 2 ·
THINK SIMPLE

Too Much Knowledge and Experience Can Overcomplicate Your Thinking

My book called *"I'm Fine" Spirit* is a collection of some of the core ideas of my teachings. As I wrote in its preface, I believe that the book can be useful to people of any age and ethnicity. It is a book that is valuable enough to be considered primary reading for everyone, and it would be a shame to read it only as a supplementary book. It is filled with teachings that can be made useful in many ways, so it can also serve as an employee handbook for your company.

Since *"I'm Fine" Spirit* covers many important points, I would like to narrow them down to just a few to discuss here. Part one talks about living with simplicity and a carefree spirit. This is a surprisingly valuable principle. Over time, our minds become overcomplicated as we learn and experience more and more new things. The more knowledge we gain, the more things there are to think about. And the more we go through a variety of experiences, the more we start to think negatively. The complexity of our lives makes us indecisive: we become stuck between choices and begin to spend a long time agonizing about what to do.

We expect to get smarter as we gain more knowledge and experience, but many people find that as they go through their thirties, forties, fifties, and sixties, they spend an increasing amount of time fretting and feeling troubled. Our thinking becomes too elaborate, and we lose the ability to simply take things as they are.

It is easier to act bravely and decisively when we are young because we are starting from a clean slate of knowledge and experience. There is nothing to hold us back. As we age, however, our courage begins to wane and we start to take a more defensive approach to life. We might hesitate to do something in a new way because we think the old ways have been working well so far and are good enough. Or we might be afraid to make a decision between two people because we are afraid of offending one of them. This is how we slowly get used to overthinking. Instead, we should make a persistent effort to keep things simple and uncomplicated. When we do so, we see our wisdom grow. We discipline ourselves to rationally accept things as they are and avoid complicating things, even as we continue to experience new things and gain new knowledge.

Clean Out the Cobwebs from Your Mind

Without regular maintenance, your mind is prone to becoming overcrowded by little cobwebs of thought. Sooner or later, you will find yourself entangled and immobilized by the array of spider webs that has collected in your mind. If you ever find yourself in this predicament, make the resolution to give your mind a good cleaning. As long as you put your mind to it, with practice, you will be able to think with more simplicity and rationality again.

Ask yourself whether there are any spider webs in your mind right now that have caught you in a trap. Does your mind feel stuck anywhere, as if you were a poor butterfly stuck to a sticky web, fluttering its wings but completely unable to escape? These spider webs are the fetters in life that weigh us down. They can be the fetters of human relationships or the problems we face at work. If you find yourself stuck in any of life's troubles, take out the broom and get rid of those cobwebs with a decisive sweep. Approach the matter rationally, and think simply.

It is actually difficult to think simply, but the results are tremendous. Thinking simply gives us the power to take action. Simplifying things will help you see what you should do and which decisions to make so you can run straight to your destination. To use a different analogy, being stuck in a spider web is like being immobilized in the thick sheets of the Antarctic ice. We have to be like icebreakers that keep tearing through the thickest ice and keep moving forward. If we ever get stuck somewhere, we have to find a way to tear the ice and plow a path.

Gracefully Abandon Lesser Things
in Favor of Higher Value

Many intelligent people become paralyzed by overly complex thinking. So from time to time, we should remember the value of being plain and positive. Just be modest and live cheerfully. Stop dwelling in and holding on to the past. Stop thinking too much about other people's feelings. Forget about your grudges and envious thoughts. Get rid of them immediately! This is simplicity.

You will learn to live gracefully by accepting things as they are and swiftly moving on. To live gracefully means many things, but in short, I believe that grace comes from the ability to let go of something completely to gain something else that has more value—even when there are countless things that we desire. Negative attachments come in many forms, and if we try too hard to have everything, we will find ourselves paralyzed throughout life. So make the decision to choose the things that are important over the others. Just let go of lesser things. You will find that your heart feels much lighter. I believe that living with simplicity and grace is a truly wise way to live.

There is no purpose in being sandwiched and paralyzed between two choices; it only results in a lot of wasted time.

Dwelling Too Long on Our Inferiority Complex Is a Form of Self-Centeredness

In our younger years, we are prone to developing inferiority complexes, and there is no one who does not have one complex or another. These childhood complexes are one of the things that we should let go of. You have spent too much time dwelling on them if at the age of fifty, sixty, or seventy, you still have the same inferiority complex you had in childhood. Somewhere along the way, we need to get rid of our complexes and change them.

This is an important part of maturing into adults. We have not fully matured into adulthood if we are still seeking people's sympathy. We are not adults yet if we still need our parents' help. True adults are those who are on the side of helping people, not on the side of being helped. Having an inferiority complex makes us very busy being so self-conscious that we have little room to think about others. We can only think about ourselves and worry about how to be saved. So if we ever find ourselves trapped within our complexes, we need to overcome them as soon as we can.

When we suffer through inferiority complexes, we are

apt to believe that our hearts are very pure and transparent and fragile like glass or crystal. If you have had this kind of self-image for many years, erase it now, because it is a distorted one. It is another form of self-centeredness. Inferiority complexes are unavoidable when we are young, but it is important not to carry them with you for so many years that they become a form of egotism and self-centeredness. Stop paying too much attention to yourself, and just shift your focus to helping other people.

Of course, there is no one in this world who is completely free from an inferiority complex, and we must all face the challenges of overcoming such feelings. The solution is simple: change yourself from someone who is troubled by your own problems into someone who helps other people find the answers to their problems. To accomplish this, it is most important to reflect upon the state of your mind.

· 3 ·

BE BRAVE
AND FACE YOUR PROBLEMS

●──────────────────────────────●

Face Your Problems Positively
and Use Them For Your Growth

Step four in *"I'm Fine" Spirit* is about being strong in the face of criticism. We should try to be positive and accept our worries, work responsibilities, and hardships in a constructive way. The purpose of being born into this world was not to live an easy life. At Happy Science, we believe that the purpose of our lives on earth is to face challenges that will help our souls advance to the next level and shine even brighter than before. If you ever feel as though life is being tough on you and you are facing too many hardships, remember that we are never given a burden that is too great for us to bear. You were given the problems you have been facing, because you have the ability to withstand them.

No matter how tough our lives become, in the final analysis, we will all pass on from this world, and all of our problems will die with us—it is that simple. We are here to spend the time that we have in accepting the problems this life gives us and using them to cultivate growth in our souls. Some of us have formed a habit of escaping from our problems. We believe that our issues are too difficult to solve, that our jobs are too demanding for us. We easily fall into the habit of saying, "I can't go on anymore," "I can't believe I have to work overtime again today," "This job is too hard for me,"—"I can't!"

Often, the habit itself of repeating these negative thoughts is what is making us unhappy. Ask yourself right now if you have a similar habit, and before you let the next negative thought slip from your lips, pause for a moment and try again to accept your problems with grace. When you think about the problem that you are facing—for example, a tough assignment at work or a difficulty in life—embrace it peacefully. Do not run away from the problem. Instead, face it with courage. Say to yourself, "I wonder why I am faced with this challenge. It must be to give me a chance to grow."

Be Brave

In the final analysis, there is not much of a difference in people's abilities. What it comes down to is our courage. Strangely enough, when we have a lot of knowledge or are in a position of power, we tend to act with less courage. This is what causes problems.

University professors make a living by spending a lot of time studying their subjects, and professors from the University of Tokyo are expected to possess more knowledge than other professors because they work at one of the best schools in Japan. Yet, ironically, those who become professors there tend to publish fewer books because they are afraid that if they publish something wrong, their reputation will suffer. They keep postponing publishing their books until they have done more research. It is difficult for them to muster enough courage to just do it. We expect that because they are intelligent people who have spent a lot of time in study, they will write many books, but the unfortunate fact is that they end up writing less and less.

A similar phenomenon occurs in many people who work in positions of authority for large companies. People with significant responsibility need to be brave and make decisions about important matters. But instead, the important papers are just added to the inbox and are never attended to. Many capable people find that because they have avoided addressing important problems, they are unable to bring excellent results to their company. This happens often in real life.

What we need is courage. It is important for everyone to be brave, for courage has the power to change us. The truth is that knowledge has limitations, and it all comes down to our courage.

THINK **BIG!**

We Can Get Through It
When We Are Pushed to the Limit

When you are entrusted with a position of power, you have to follow through on your responsibilities. It was in November 2007 that I myself took courage and went overseas to give a lecture in English.* It happened to be just one month after I had given a lecture† on my book *The Starting Point of Youth*‡, in which I wrote that even though I have spent a lot of time studying English, I am still unable to use the language freely and fluently. Lo and behold, I was giving a lecture overseas in English the very next month. I learned that we really never know what will happen in life.

I had never gone overseas to give a lecture in English before. For the first time in my life, I had to stand in front of a foreign audience and deliver a talk in English. Since I am the founder of Happy Science, I could not run away from my responsibility. So I made the decision to not worry about how well or poorly I speak in English. I said to myself that what mattered most was that the audience under-stand the gist of my message. I say from my personal experience that when you are in a position of responsibil-

---

* The lecture "Be Positive" was held at the Hawaii Branch of Happy Science on November 18, 2007.
† The earlier lecture was titled "Never Lose Your 'Hungry Spirit.'"
‡ See Ryuho Okawa, *Seishun No Genten* [The Starting Point of Youth] (Tokyo: IRH Press, 2007).

ity, there is no turning back! You have to take courage.

To some, it may have seemed odd for someone with imperfect English skills to give a lecture to people who speak it perfectly. In the Q & A session, the native speakers of course spoke perfect English, and I also noticed that the Japanese who had spent ten or twenty years abroad spoke very fluently, too. They sounded just like the native speakers and were far better than I was. So you see, regardless of my language skills, it is my job to deliver lectures. This is my profession, and professionals should never run away from their duties. Once that job comes to you, there are no excuses, and there is no turning back.

Somehow, I was able to pull off my lecture in Hawaii, even though I had only three days to practice my English. It had been more than twenty years since I used English at a previous job. So for more than ten hours a day, for three days, I listened to nothing but English and then went straight to Hawaii. Even in such a short amount of time, I found that it was not impossible to do something if I put my mind to it. This experience taught me that we humans can accomplish anything when we are placed in a position of no turning back!

Once I gave it a try, I discovered that I can manage to give talks in English, and soon, I was giving many more of them. Interestingly, I found that the people who listen to my English lectures believe that I speak English well, when in fact, they speak the language far better than I do. This happens because I have a wealth of experience in public speaking, having given well over 2,400 lectures* in Japanese. I am a well-seasoned professional in the art of giving talks, regardless of the level of my English skills. On the other hand, younger members of Happy Science's staff have a difficult time giving English lectures, even though their language skills are more advanced than mine, because they lack experience. This is how it works in reality, and in the end, we all simply need to take courage.

Use Positive Self-Affirmations
to Motivate and Encourage Yourself

I believe that in this age, increasing numbers of people will continue to change jobs and even begin learning new languages in their forties, fifties, and even sixties and beyond. When you start working at a new place, you will probably have completely new things to learn. Let's be honest: everyone has at least some fear when facing jobs with which they have no experience. It is not so difficult to start something new in your twenties, but it can be quite tough to work in a new field when you are in your sixties.

However, I would like for everyone to have self-confi-

---

* As of February 2016.

dence and to keep motivating and encouraging themselves. If you have previous experience as a department manager overseeing, say, fifty employees, you already have many valuable skills and executive experience in management and decision-making. Even if you were to start all over at a new company, it should not take long for your performance to surpass that of any of the entry-level employees.

Believe in the tremendous power of self-affirmation. The spirit of the "I'm Fine" principle also applies here. We should constantly and repeatedly give ourselves positive self-affirmations; we should say to ourselves, "I'm completely fine! I can do it! I can definitely do this!" The more we convince ourselves that nothing is impossible, the more we will achieve. We are never too old to start over!

It is important not to complain too much. If you keep making excuses and saying, "I can't do this; I can't do that," you will only hinder your ability to achieve. So instead, make affirmations. Say, "I can do it!" and "I will learn how to do this!"

Use the Power of Habit

I have found that you are never too old to start exercising. Our physical fitness has nothing to do with our age. When I go out for my walks, I often bump into an elderly gentleman. He must be over eighty years old, but he can walk so fast that he zips right past me. This is not a joke; I would need a bicycle to keep up with him! I would estimate his walking speed to be more than 3.5 miles per hour. Many people, even at advanced ages, still have strong healthy legs. On the other hand, some people in their twenties are out of breath at the slightest incline. What is the difference between these people and the older men and women who walk briskly uphill? It is exercise. Daily exercise will build strong healthy legs, no matter how old or young we are.

What they are using in their exercise is the power of habit. In the final analysis, people who successfully develop good habits are the ones who come out on top, whether in sports or in studies. You need to use willpower in the beginning, but once you have created good habits and practiced them over and over, they will transform into power before you know it. If we look at learning English, for example, if you get into the habit of memorizing ten new words every day, it won't take long before you notice that you have built a stronger vocabulary. If you spend thirty minutes to an hour walking every day, your legs will become stronger before you know it. This principle applies to everything. If you wish to master the "I'm fine" spirit, use the power of habit to keep encouraging yourself to become more positive and energetic, and I assure you that your wish will eventually come true.

· 4 ·

GENERATING YOUR OWN POWER

Make the Effort to Radiate Positivity

Step seven of *"I'm Fine" Spirit* is about making the effort to radiate positivity all the time. Our friends will begin to leave us if all we do is talk about negative ideas. No one wants to be around messengers of doom. So instead of saying, for example, "Something bad is going to happen to me," "Our business is going to fail," or "The world is going to get worse," try to radiate positivity. We all like people who are cheerful, because we feel energized when we spend time with them. If negative words have a habit of slipping from your lips, make a strong effort to stop them. Even teenagers can fall into this bad habit, but pessimism tends to become more of a habit as we age.

Of course, this is often caused by physical fatigue and emotional trauma. Still, this does not change the fact that everyone wants to stay away from pessimistic people. So we should make an honest effort to give off positive, constructive energy. If it rains, for example, some people may think, "What a terrible rainy day! Rainy days make me feel so groggy." But positive people will say, "I am proud that I am encouraging myself to study even though it is a rainy day!" And compare someone who thinks, "I can't believe that I can't go out during my vacation!" to someone who says, "This vacation is the perfect time for me to study! I'm proud of myself for making an effort when everyone else is going out to have fun." The latter person certainly deserves our praise.

Be a Person of Light, Not of Gloom

When you begin to get the hang of thinking positive, you will learn to help yourself; that is, you will learn to generate your own energy. It is my hope that all people will become self-generators. We should make it our goal to have the power to light ourselves up, make ourselves glow, and shine our inner light brightly. It is an unavoidable fact that the world is full of darkness and we are constantly surrounded by an abundance of negative energy. So my dream is to create as many people as possible who have the power inside them to shine brilliantly in the gloom.

In the final analysis, what matters most is each and every person's ability to generate his or her own inner light and cast a brilliant glow. I have given many lectures to help as many people as possible find ways to shine brightly, but it is impossible for me to help the whole world shine, all on my own. This is why I would like to teach people how to generate their own light. Once people come to understand my teachings, I am sure that they will be able to light their own inner candles.

And when, in time, you learn to maintain a positive, constructive, and cheerful attitude, no matter what trials come your way, it means that I have managed to save one person out of the seven billion people on Earth. I am sure that once you have achieved this for yourself, you will move on to saving the people around you, too.

My dream is to light up this world. What is this light that I speak of? This light is the opposite of darkness. It is the power to dispel gloom. Then what is darkness? Darkness symbolizes ignorance of the Truths, complaints, feelings of discontent, and excessive desire. When we look inside our mind and find it filled with an unsightly muddiness, that is what I mean by darkness.

We should never become dark people. Instead, our aim should be to become people of light. If you suffer from discontent and a lot of complaining, you should realize that your state of mind is attuned to Hell right now, and you should try to find a way out of that dark world. It will be too late if you wait until you pass on from this world and find yourself in the dark underworld. So start looking for the way out immediately.

Stop Making Excuses

What is the way out? First, you must develop the right mindset. To do this, you should begin by sowing good seeds in your mind. Then, you should consistently adopt the right way of thinking and cultivate a constructive attitude that you will always keep in mind. Finally, you have to take right action. If you have time to complain, ask yourself whether you can spend that time engaged in more constructive, positive, courageous actions.

I would especially like to emphasize that we should not look for excuses about why we cannot do something. Instead, it is important to look for ways to move forward, inch by inch. It is a sign that we have become too clever if we find ourselves making excuses before we even try. Many people start doing this as they get older, and intelligent people are prone to this habit. So if you notice that you are making excuses more frequently, take a moment to reflect, make the decision to stop, try to be more constructive, and search for ways to move forward instead.

There is nothing productive in explaining to your boss your reasons why a job cannot be completed. But those who search for and suggest ways to make improvements will be able to help save their company in times of recession and develop their company in times of stability. All companies are looking for people who represent positivity in tough times, because those are very valuable people.

Often, we become less and less energetic as we age. However, if you are able to remain energetic even as you get older, you should have no problems making a career change. But a job change may be difficult for you if your energy diminishes. That is all there is to it. Some of us may keep making excuses like, "It is the system that is wrong and preventing older people from finding jobs," or "So many of us are part of the working poor; the world is just full of hardship," or "It's the government's fault. There is something wrong with the world." But the truth might be that we just need to change our attitude. So begin by changing your attitude, your habits, the things you say, and your way of thinking.

Mumblers Will Not Find Love

An old Japanese saying says that the love of mumblers will not be requited. This may be too old a quote for younger generations to be familiar with. Mumblers are people who are so defeatist about themselves that they tell the people around them that they are worthless and that the object of their love will probably reject them. People with this habit of foretelling their own doom are not usually lucky in love, and believe me, there are many of them. They are only trying to avoid getting hurt. It is like laying down a gym mat so that there is something to catch you in case you fall; they are trying to protect themselves from rejection. And then when their love is not accepted, they only have to say, "I knew this was going to happen. I'm glad I prepared myself for it."

People with this mindset will not have much luck in love, so if you are one of them, please change your attitude right away. Of course, the chances of rejection may be high for a young man who confesses his love or proposes marriage to a woman. But the man should put himself in the woman's shoes. Women often appreciate being approached, regardless of whether or not they want to accept a man's advances, and many of them are wishing that you would at least give them the chance to decline. And while some women may not return your love, others are actually waiting for the man to approach them so they can accept him. Unfortunately, many women are attracted to a certain man and are disappointed that he never approaches her because he has given up before even trying. They wish that he would have given them a chance to reject him once or even to reject him three times until she is ready to accept him on his fourth try. Women would also like to be given the chance to choose, and men should graciously offer them the opportunity to do so.

If you adopt this perspective, you will see that it is not such a bad thing to be rejected. If it happens to you, you did a gentlemanly deed and gave a woman the opportunity to choose. I hope that more men will be braver and give more women an opportunity to decline a man's courtship.

Nothing Can Be Accomplished Without Repeatedly Challenging Ourselves

If we do not challenge ourselves again and again, we will never be able to accomplish anything. This is true of our jobs. During our younger years, more often than not, the ideas we propose at the workplace will not be accepted no matter how many suggestions we offer our superiors. However, if you do not give up and continue to propose your ideas, your persistence is sure to impress them.

Many superiors will immediately reject your ideas at first, regardless of the quality of your proposal. They may say to you, "This is still your first year here," or "You've only been working three years with us," or "Aren't you getting ahead of yourself?" Your superiors may do this if they notice that you have a precocious personality and worry that accepting your input could incite jealousy among your senior colleagues.

Therefore, even if your superior dismisses your idea with a loud "no," you should not take it to heart. Don't give up, and keep insisting assertively. If you are the most persistent one, then no one will have a reason to complain if your superior decides to accept your idea in the end. So if you ever find that your opinion is rejected, remember that it could be because immediately accepting an idea from a new employee could invite jealousy from older colleagues who might then harass you. This may be especially likely to happen to you if you have a lot of potential to grow and become successful in the future. Your superior might intentionally try to push you away by saying, "That's a useless idea," or "A college student could come up with an idea like that. You need to up your game in the real world." Your superior might say things like this as a kind of test to rough you up a bit and see how you cope with it.

Accomplished people in positions of power are sometimes hoping that their subordinates will say to themselves, "You wait and see, I'm not going to give up!" and keep returning to them with their ideas, over and over again. They are always on the lookout for employees with a strong backbone.

The same principles that can help a man approach a woman can also apply in our careers. If you think that your ideas are good or right, then keep coming back with them. If you often make excuses or run away from your problems, please make a constant effort to change your life to a positive and constructive one. By doing so, I am sure that you will achieve success gracefully.

3

THINK BIG!

· 1 ·

YOUR WAY OF THINKING
IS POWERFUL

The Japanese Should Realize
that Your Way of Thinking Is Powerful

It might seem obvious that we should "think big," but when you think about it, no one ever tells us that it is valuable to think big—not at school, and not even at the workplace. Even if we happen to stumble across this idea in a book, it may feel like an idea that has little relevance to our lives— an idea for people in a distant world rather than an idea for us. Indeed, many of us probably have very little under- standing of what thinking big is about.

But surprisingly, there are entire shelves in bookstores all around the United States that are full of books about thinking big. This goes to show the huge demand that Americans have for this way of thinking. In contrast, very few books of this kind are sold in Japan, and I believe that the Japanese have not yet discovered the hidden power within this mindset.

Americans understand the tremendous power that is

housed in the way we think. The United States is a mobile society that has long been a haven for immigrants from all over the world who seek out this land of opportunity. People know that in America, they will have a chance to build a positive future through hard work and effort, and they know that this land provides many opportunities for upward mobility. In comparison, the force of conformity is deeply rooted in Japan, and those who stand out from the pack are hammered down under the pressure of uniformity.

I have asked myself what could be at the root of this equalizing force, and I have come to the conclusion that it must be jealousy. It is part of human nature to feel jealous when we see a peer advance further than us. We also become nervous out of a fear of jealous eyes when we ourselves get ahead of others, so we keep our head down as much as we can. In this modern age, the idea that we can evade trouble by avoiding standing out is deeply rooted in Japanese society. I believe that this mentality has manifested in the frequent intentional destruction of the bubble economy; jealousy has been a constant force that has dragged down and destroyed successful people. Character may be an important factor, but our mental attitudes have an enormous impact on our lives. Many people still do not realize just how powerful our mental attitude is.

I Learned to Think Big
through the Positive Thinking Philosophy

As a teenager, I was always talking about big dreams and huge ideals every time I opened my mouth. But in contrast to my outward personality, on the inside I was insecure, constantly criticizing myself and thinking about my failures, putting myself down for my weaknesses, mulling over people's criticisms about me, and dwelling on all the things that were not going well in my life. I carried on this way until I was in my early twenties. But when I encountered the New Thought philosophy, I began to make a thorough study of thinking big, and I changed my mindset completely. I made a decisive turn in my way of thinking once I was able to fully understand the mindset of positive thinking.

Until this dramatic turning point in my life, I used to worry about what people said about me. I was always dwelling over small insecurities, pointlessly worrying about the future, and dragging negative events from the past with me into the present. I was terrified of making an embarrassment of myself in front of other people, and I was too hopelessly shy to speak to people. Whenever I tried to talk to someone, I would get so nervous and my heart would pound so quickly that I was afraid I was going to have a heart attack. But today, my position has reversed, and many people who come to my lectures get very nervous in front of me. It is amazing how completely my life has turned around since then. I have become the exact opposite of who I used to be. This taught me that what we are thinking about all the time has a tremendous impact on our lives.

I spent a great deal of time studying the American New Thought thinkers, and I discovered that many of these philosophers experienced huge setbacks in their early lives, either in childhood or later on, into their thirties. It was through a period of adversity that they discovered clues about life that eventually opened their eyes and led them to a complete turnaround. Most of them either faced an important failure or suffered deeply from an inferiority complex. Some had illnesses or were in car accidents. Others had family circumstances that led to an inferiority complex—they may have faced poverty or fallen short of the level of academic achievement they desired. They may have failed in getting a job, failed in a romantic relationship, or gone through troubles in marriage. Others had difficulties in raising their children or went through difficult career changes. Stories like these are so common that they exist everywhere, but very few have been able to grasp the essential truth from within these setbacks and find the strength to get back up again. I deeply admire the strength and valor of those who grasped hold of the law of success that was hidden in their hardships and found the courage to pull themselves up once more.

The Disparity Between My Self-Assessment and People's Assessment of Me

During my early twenties, I had a confident outward personality, but on the inside I was extremely sensitive and easily hurt. In time, I learned that people's true nature is always defined by their thoughts and the things they are constantly thinking about—not by their outward presentation or physical appearance. When I realized that I am what I am always thinking about, experienced this truth for myself, and internalized it within me, I began to change.

Even then, I did not think highly of myself at all. I continued to have low self-esteem, while the people around me saw me in a completely different light. I remember very well that this discrepancy between my self-image and the positive evaluations of my colleagues and superiors never really disappeared. I believe that this was due to the fact that I had a strong tendency toward perfectionism that began in childhood. I tended to brood over small mistakes, and I had a difficult time letting them go from my mind. Because I could not be satisfied with anything but perfection, this tendency created a poor self-image.

I so stubbornly adhered to this self-perception that the gap between my own perception of myself and others' perceptions of me often led to misunderstandings. When I was twenty-seven or twenty-eight years old, I was transferred to a different department in the company where I was working, and I was instructed to do something that completely surprised me. I was told repeatedly, "When you start working at the new department, no matter what you do, don't work too hard. Relax, sit still, and do nothing." This was a shocking thing to be told, and for a while, I could not believe my ears! I would have been excited to work hard if they had told me, "Good luck, and give it your best effort," but I was dumbfounded to be told to do nothing at all. "No one thinks that you're not a competent person. So just sit still, and don't ever try to show how much you are capable of."

Even as I disbelieved my ears, I tried to follow their advice. For six months, I relaxed as much as I could and did as little work as I could allow myself to do. To my astonishment, my reputation got better and better. This was beyond my understanding. I was the kind of person who always worked hard but was rarely satisfied with my performance and continually strove for improvement. But I followed the advice they gave me. I held back, did not work too hard, and relaxed. To my complete bewilderment, my reputation improved. Through this experience, I came to understand that Japanese society functioned in a strange way. In Japan, when I adhered to my own standards with as much integrity as possible and pushed myself to the limit of my abilities, it gave my colleagues the impression that I was telling them they were incompetent. It was my nature to set high standards for myself, and I was never satisfied until I had given my work my best effort. But to my surprise, this caused my colleagues to feel as if I was trying to show them that they were robbing the company of their salary. This had never occurred to me before, and it was not at all my intention. I was only trying to carry out my work at a level that I thought would be satisfactory. It took me some time to get over the shock I received from being evaluated positively by making so little effort.

Japan and the United States
Value Your Abilities Differently

Before this bewildering event, I used to work in the United States. There, if I had ever pretended to be less competent than I really was, no one would have questioned it, and my performance would have been evaluated poorly. In the United States, you have to be able to say, "Yes, I can," to be accepted as a competent member of the organization. Americans can immediately tell how capable you are and are very quick to acknowledge people's abilities. People are rarely given acknowledgement in Japanese society, but Americans will tell you right away if they think highly of your competence.

In America, for example, if I was working with my

coworkers, my superior would walk right up and ask the others to leave to allow us to talk privately. Americans have a way of being straightforward and businesslike with which I was very comfortable. Thanks to the American culture, my relationships in the United States always went well; I always felt at ease speaking up and expressing my opinions straightforwardly.

Things were very different in Japan, however. There is a Japanese saying: "A skillful hawk hides its talons." In Japan, working too hard is often interpreted as self-centeredness. As a result, we need to play down our skills and present ourselves as having mediocre abilities. Working hard to appear average is perceived as "hiding our talons"—it is considered a virtuous character trait. Despite what I learned over the years, I never found this to be a fulfilling way to work. My desire to set higher standards and reach farther toward self-perfection never disappeared.

· 2 ·

THE SIZE OF YOUR ACHIEVEMENTS IS DETERMINED BY YOUR WAY OF THINKING

I Could Not Have Confidence until I Grasped the Larger Perspective

It was my nature that I didn't feel confident until I had a grasp of the big picture—and so it went with my job. If I were competing in a swimming race, I would be the swimmer that would start speeding up only when my head surfaced after the first few meters. So in anything I ventured into, I always felt as if I was getting nowhere in the initial stages. As soon as I could get a hold of the larger perspective, though, things started to move very quickly.

There was such a deviation between my own self-image and the perception of people around me that I was constantly left stupefied. For example, when I authored several books of Truth and published them through a small publisher, they were amazed by my books' stellar sales performance. Never before had they published such a successful book. As for my own reaction, I was bewildered to find out that selling ten thousand to fifteen thousand copies meant a huge success to them. I never imagined that such a performance would be considered a successful one.

It is true that objectively speaking, very few books sell ten thousand copies, including those from large publishers. On average, most books do not sell more than three thousand copies, and that's usually the point at which they break even. So all publishers, large and small, are always on the lookout for books with the potential to sell ten thousand copies; a title that sells ten to twenty thousand copies is considered a bestseller. All of my books have sold that many copies, but since new authors rarely sell that well in the beginning, the publisher was very pleasantly surprised.

In contrast, I myself was not very satisfied with the results. Based on my personal standards, I didn't think I could claim that my book had done well until it sold over a million copies. I did eventually learn that from a publishing perspective, a million copies is an astronomical number that very rarely occurs, especially without a very clever marketing strategy. A while ago, the CEO of a publishing company said that a book never sells millions of copies unless it is released in paperback form in combination with a movie and the book is also advertised with the film. Since I had always believed that a bestseller had to sell a million copies, I realized that there was a disparity between my perception and the perception of the rest of the world.

THINK **BIG!**

You Will Not Achieve Big If You Think Small

In the majority of cases when I failed at something, it was because I overextended myself. I often aimed so far that the people around me had difficulty understanding what I was trying to do. This was the case both before and after I founded Happy Science. My remedy for handling this situation was very simple: I relaxed and remained low-key for some time until my reputation improved again.

In the end, however, your achievements will never grow beyond your aims. If you think too small, you will never be able to achieve big. If you are satisfied with an average salary that will let you get by and provide a stable life, then you may simply aim to get along well with everyone and avoid drawing too much attention to yourself. However, if you want to make your life worthwhile, make it big in some way, achieve excellence in your field, become an entrepreneur, or do something that attracts the world's recognition, then you should always keep in mind that you will never achieve more than what you picture in your mind.

People who have high aspirations may struggle with the disparity between themselves and those around them. They may face friction with others or become the target of criticism. But thinking small means that deep down, you do not have a desire for huge success. There are some exceptions when thinking small leads to success, but generally speaking, over the long term, thinking small will not lead anyone down the path of success.

· **3** ·

HAVE HIGH ASPIRATIONS AND WORK STEADILY

● ── ●

High Achievers in Examinations
Have a Habit of Thinking Negatively

The greatest weakness of intelligent people who achieve excellent exam scores is the habit of thinking negatively. This mindset ensures that they will not feel disappointed when their scores are returned, because their scores will be higher than they expected. This pessimism comes from having a strong fear of getting points taken off for wrong answers. The better someone is at taking exams, the more likely it is that they have this habit. Today's bureaucrats have a very bad reputation, because most of them have this trait. Thinking negatively and assuming the worst have become such an ingrained habit that they have trained themselves to focus on minimizing damage when they should be creating constructive results.

When someone asks, "How do you think you did on your exam?" people like them will usually reply, "I did horribly. I might get the worst score this time." When their exams are returned, however, their scores are usually very high. It feels good to them to use this trick, because they think it will impress their peers: "You said it went horribly, but look how well you did!" It gives the impression that they must be very intelligent people. We should not allow this mindset to continue into adulthood, however, because it will develop into a habit of always aiming low.

Of course, setting high goals means being disappointed when you fail to reach them. But there is nothing wrong with spending a long time chasing after lofty goals and never reaching them. Setting your goals low may give you the temporary fulfillment of being able to say, "My successes always surpass my expectations." But if you are satisfied with having small ambitions, you will become accustomed to taking the easy path. Unfortunately, this is not the path to real success.

Therefore, if you find that you are achieving your goals without much trouble, you should determine to set your aspirations much higher. It should not matter if you never reach them, because what is valuable is the experiences from which you can learn and grow as you keep challenging your potential.

Set Your Goals High,
Even If the Risk of Failure Is High

Even if you think big, you are not going to see the results you want right away. But if you think small from the start, you will never achieve extraordinary things. So we should set ourselves high aspirations and keep working toward them surely and steadily.

The Happiness Realization Party, a political party supported by Happy Science, ran in the Upper House elections in 2010. We had a full year for our campaign activities, in contrast to the 2009 Lower House elections, which gave us only three months. In spite of the longer time we spent campaigning in 2010, our district results only totaled half the votes we had received in the Lower House election the year before. We spent much more time and effort in 2010, so what were the reasons for such a poor outcome compared with the previous year? We could probably think of an array of causes, but I think the main reason had to do with our strategy. The Happiness Realization Party adopted the idea that "a small leak can sink a great ship" and so focused on a small number of candidates. But I had the opposite perspective. If the party's goal is just to drill a small hole so that one candidate might make it through the ship's wall, that leaves the candidates feeling like tiny ants. This thinking is too small.

The people of Japan are not going to resonate with our

ideals if our party is aiming for small goals. The Japanese citizens were not moved or inspired by our party's aspirations. If you set your goals low, you will have a smaller risk of making large mistakes, and you will not have to be responsible for anything big. This strategy is a safe one that minimizes possible failures. But it is not one that will inspire a lot of people to support the party.

The Happiness Realization Party was founded only recently, in 2009, to run in the Lower House election held that year. Although we were complete novices, we still set our goals as high as possible, aiming to be Japan's leading party. As a result, we received a total of 1,070,000 votes in the single-seat districts. In comparison, we garnered only 230,000 votes in the district blocs in 2010, which clearly showed that our small thinking limited our success. Without a doubt, we would have received more votes if we had continued to pursue the same goals we pursued in the 2009 campaign.

Setting goals that minimize our chances of failure and maximize our chances of success may be a good strategy for an office worker that wants to avoid getting into trouble. But this way of thinking only makes sense for employees in large companies and government bureaucrats who want to evade responsibility. If you adopt this mentality as an entrepreneur seeking to establish your own business, you will have difficulty attracting support. You need to think much bigger than that. And while you keep hold of the bigger perspective, you need to surely and steadily continue to work toward your goals.

In conclusion, I believe that the main reason the Happiness Realization Party did so poorly in 2010 was because its ambitions were small. Since our goal was only to fulfill the requirements of the Political Party Public Subsidy Act, an entire year of preparation resulted in only a small number of votes. We gave the Japanese people the impression that we were a completely unenthusiastic party. We need to create a much more ambitious strategy in the future.

We tried to run the Happiness Realization Party independently from Happy Science, and this may have caused a lack of cooperation between the two organizations. It is true that Happy Science dedicated only 10 percent of its energy to supporting the party. But in the final analysis, I have to say that our mistake was in thinking too small. We should not have used the strategy of trying to sink a ship by creating a small hole. Instead, we should have aimed to surge through like a colossal wave. By setting our goals high, we will face a higher risk of failing and will also be subjected to other negative consequences, but as long as we avoid taking this risk, there will be little room for ourselves and our endeavors to grow.

What We Think About for a Long Time
Will Eventually Be Actualized

Happy Science has grown large now, but I often find that my ideas have not yet reached everyone. Small thinking keeps infiltrating our organization. Many people who work for Happy Science originally came from other companies and brought with them their previous employers' cultures. So they tend to interpret my ideas on a much smaller scale than I intend. They also tend to train our younger staff based on the kind of education they received in their previous jobs, and I feel that this is restraining many members of our staff from working at their full potential. As for myself, it is not my nature to wring my subordinates' necks about small matters or be very strict in training them about small things. So it has often been my experience that my ideas are not fully understood.

This fundamental law never changes: you will never become bigger than the size of your aspirations. But it is a fact that if you keep thinking about your aspirations long enough, they will eventually come true. I achieved great enlightenment more than thirty years ago, and I was all alone at first, with the exception of the voices that frequently visited me from Heaven. This was a very lonely period in my life. I remember feeling as helpless as a spider dangling from its thread. I had no followers to support me, and I could not imagine finding support from anyone at work. This was how it all started.

Today, I have built many *shojas** around Japan. There are over six hundred branches and locations nationwide, and we will keep growing toward one thousand. We have established approximately one hundred branches and locations overseas, and we are aiming to expand into two hundred countries worldwide.[†] We continue to release our own movies and publish many books. Meanwhile, we have also built the Happy Science Academy. As I mentioned before, we also founded the Happiness Realization Party, which is aiming to become Japan's leading party. When I look back, we are clearly doing it all. This is my proof to you of the tremendous power of our thoughts.

As of now, none of our nominees has been elected to office in the national elections yet, but my opinions and ideas have powerfully influenced the Japanese government's decisions as well as the bureaucracy and the mass media, which have leverage over the government. This influence can only grow and will never weaken. My achievements are the result of my persistent effort, often made gradually in the shadows, despite having been told to do as little work as possible and avoid drawing attention to myself.

---

* *Shojas* are large centers of faith where Happy Science followers gather.
† As of February, 2016.

· 4 ·

CREATE A FUTURE OF PROSPERITY THROUGH THE POWER OF YOUTH

● ──────────────────────────── ●

What You Studied in Your Twenties
Will Equip You With Power

Knowledge is power. My experiences have taught me that knowing is powerful. What you study and thoroughly digest, especially during your twenties, will equip you with tremendous power. The things I learned and the books that I read during my college years and the several years after graduation have remained in my memory most vividly and have become the building blocks of my abilities. Of course, I have continued to read many books since then, but my recollection of them is much more faded. Without doubt, the things I read and learned in my twenties played the most significant role in building my character. Until your twenties, your growth is mainly determined by the food you eat, but in your twenties, what you read and learn gives your soul the nourishment it needs to grow into the next stage.

To Become a Leading Nation,
Japan Must Produce Many Successful People

Since the Democratic Party of Japan took office, Japan has started to backtrack toward a shrinking mentality. This administration is trying to push everything down. It is trying to create a world of uniformity based on lowered standards. Like a tire jack, I have been opposing this downward trend by warning the Japanese people of this nation's movement toward mediocrity. It has been quite a heavy load to lift, but I am doing my best to breathe as much life back into our country as possible. If I divert my attention, our nation will begin to decline again.

I believe that the future of Japan depends on its younger generations. It is young people who can build a nation of prosperity. Do not give in to your fears, and stay brave in this endeavor. We need to get rid of the culture of jealousy that drags down the successful and the prosperous. We need to create a country that produces one successful person after another, for otherwise, we will never become a leading nation.

Never feel guilty about success. Never give in to the kind of thinking that discourages success as an evil. When you achieve success, remember that success has valuable by-products. We call our donations at Happy Science "happiness planting," because there are many ways of making offerings that are not monetary. There is no limit to the variety of ways that we can contribute good to the world. So if you become successful in the future, do not forget your duty of sharing the fruits of your success with the rest of the world. The more success you achieve, the larger the gift you will be able to give.

Many prosperous people in the United States set up foundations to work for good causes. For example, John D. Rockefeller's success made him one of the wealthiest people of the world, but he suffered so deeply from public criticism that he became very ill in his fifties and came dangerously close to death. This was when he was inspired to use his wealth for the good of the world. He began his philanthropic work, which later led him to create the Rockefeller Foundation. His foundation used his enormous fortune to build schools and hospitals in many impoverished countries.

His health was restored to him as he began to use his private fortune for the good of the world. He lived with vitality well into his nineties. He went through very tough times during which he was assailed by public criticism, but once he began to "plant the seeds of happiness," his health made a complete turnaround. He was youthful again and even gained the gift of longevity. The price of being successful includes a responsibility to help the greater society, but there is no sin at all in success itself. Never give in to these ideas. If you possess talents or abilities, you should always aim to use them to their full potential.

Ask Not What You Were Able to Avoid, But What You Achieved

I hope that all young people will learn from my advice. Every individual faces unique problems and circumstances, and what is most important is that no matter what we are faced with, we continue to dream big. We received the gift of life, so we might as well think big, and live life to its full potential.

Only the defeated would say that life is about avoiding criticism. Some people might pride themselves in never being spoken ill of. But I believe that never being criticized in life is the same as never having accomplished anything. No one will have anything to criticize about someone who has never achieved anything. But the successful will always be assailed by criticism. The key to Heaven is not in what you were able to avoid doing, but what you were able to accomplish. When you pass on from this world, you will be asked, "What were you able to achieve in your life?" You will ultimately be judged not on what you were able to avoid, but on what you achieved.

4

THE WAY
TO SUCCESS

· 1 ·

A BOY WHO STUDIED HARD
AND WORKED HARD

● ──────────────────────────────── ●

The Tale of the Ugly Duckling
Gave Me Hope as a Child

This chapter is not just for those who are young in years, but also for everyone who is young at heart. Once upon a time, there was a boy who took an IQ test in preparation for moving up from kindergarten to primary school.* Since he believed that the test was based on a one-hundred-point system, he was thrilled to see that he scored 97. Convinced that he did excellent on the test, he ran home to tell his parents. But when his parents began to cry, he realized that something was wrong. One hundred points on the IQ test was not the maximum, but just an average score.

His older brother, who was four years his senior, had scored a very high 187. The first time he had taken the

---

* This story was a pun on Hiroshi Okawa's speech about his own childhood, which began, "Once upon a time, there was a boy who had an IQ of over 180..." In truth, Ryuho Okawa has gotten genius-level IQ scores several times.

test, he scored 186 and was asked to take the test again because his score had come out much too high. A graduate student from the education department at Tokushima University came to give him another test, and that time he performed even better and got 187. But the little brother's IQ came out to a disappointing 97.

What would become of this child? His parents expected very little from him as a student and gave him a lot of weeding and house chores to do throughout his elementary school years. They believed that it would be too difficult for him to make a living in an academic field, so they encouraged him to pursue a career in business. All through his childhood, everyone around him talked to him about how exciting it is to make money. This was how he was raised, while his older brother with twice his IQ was encouraged to study hard and pursue a career in the academic world. As a result, the younger brother went through his elementary school years with a strong inferiority complex.

In his final years of elementary school, however, this boy's grades began to improve. He started to study very enthusiastically. But as a result of focusing on his studies, he got much less exercise than he used to. The scale showed that he gained a great deal of weight; in sixth grade, at just 4 feet, 10 inches, he already weighed 143 pounds. His mother perhaps interpreted the Japanese saying "The larger will serve for the smaller" literally and bought this boy a jacket that had been made for someone who was 6 feet and 175 pounds. He looked very lumpy in his over-sized jacket. When he walked along the streets, he almost felt disgusted by the appearance of his unsightly shadow. The boy could not stop thinking about the tale of the ugly duckling.

The tale of the ugly duckling never left the mind of this boy. He thought about it over and over as it became a source of his hope that some day, the shadow of the ugly duckling would transform into a beautiful swan.

Much later on, he found out that he had written his answers on the wrong page of the IQ test. He had mis-understood the teacher's instructions and skipped an entire page of the test. His test score was so low because many of his answers had not matched up with the right questions. During the test, the boy had wondered why the teacher continued to give instructions when the test was already over. He did not understand.

In the end, he found out that his IQ was not that low, after all. But children readily believe what they are told by their parents, and for a very long time, this boy was convinced that his intelligence was below average, even though he got good grades in school. Beginning in the sixth grade, he developed a strong work ethic, because he believed that he needed to study very hard to catch up with his peers. He told himself, "If I study three times longer than the others, I might be able to catch up with them." This was the kind of attitude he developed as he grew up.

We Change Over Time

As the boy went through high school, he began to wonder why his parents gave him so little recognition for his accomplishments but heaped praise on his older brother and seemed to put him on a pedestal. The boy thought this was strange. Perhaps, he thought, it is their way of sticking to something they established a long time ago. Nowadays, when he looks back, he realizes that it could have been their way of following the Confucian order of seniority: to keep order by giving the older son higher status than his younger brother. Thankfully, due to the fact that he never thought of himself as especially bright, this boy learned to work hard and steadily in his studies.

This boy was me.

The moral of the story is: you never know what will become of a person. There are any number of exams that people may use to judge you, but people change over time. I learned through my own experiences that what really matters is the attitude of mind that you cultivate. I grew up with this philosophy. Even through my college years, my parents continued to insist that I was not intelligent at all. I supposed that they must be right, and I continued to believe them.

This actually led to my being heavily attacked by a weekly magazine when I was thirty-four, several years after I had started Happy Science at the age of thirty. They wrote that there must be something wrong in my saying that I am not intelligent when I have a law degree from the University of Tokyo.

The reason for the criticism evaded me at first, but this event taught me that there is an unwritten code not taught in school that gives people the right to criticize those who are successful. Once people gain public recognition, they become public figures, which allows the press to write negative articles about them. As I revealed before, this weekly magazine was being influenced by the Devil.* Since I never expected anything like these attacks, the first one came as a big surprise to me. It has been twenty years since this event.

I took their criticism humbly, and since then, have been careful about saying that I am unintelligent. Deep down, I still believed my parents and continued to carry an inferiority complex, but I realized the I lacked an objective awareness about how the public saw me.

---

* See Ryuho Okawa, *Shūkanshi Ni Sukuu Akuma No Kenkyū* [Investigating the Devil That Is Controlling a Weekly Magazine] (Tokyo: IRH Press, 2011).

· 2 ·

DIAMONDS MIGHT BE LYING BENEATH YOUR FEET

A Legend about How a Speaker Became Rich

It is difficult for most people to know what talents are hidden within them, how much talent they have, and what they can do to make their potential blossom. In the early twentieth century, an American speaker became extremely rich by giving more than five thousand talks in which he told the following story.

An Iranian farmer (or in some versions of the story, an Indian farmer) bought a patch of land and began digging, looking for a diamond mine. He kept digging but never found it. He ended up selling the land to someone else for a very cheap price and set out on a journey to find a diamond mine somewhere else. He traveled everywhere, but he never found one and eventually drowned near the coast of Spain.

Meanwhile, the man who bought the land from him decided to keep digging where the farmer had left off. Lo and behold, this man discovered a layer of several acres of diamonds just three inches below the spot where the farmer had stopped digging. If the man who drowned on the coast of Spain had kept digging just three more inches, he would have discovered that layer of diamonds.

Since there are several versions of this story, it is very likely to have been true. An American speaker became a millionaire by telling this story to a paying audience more than five thousand times. This is truly an example of the American dream come true.

You can probably guess the moral of the story of these two diamond miners. Most people give up just inches before their success. So many of us are like the man who would have found diamonds had he dug only three inches farther but who instead gave up. He believed that there were no diamonds where he was digging and so went on to search for another piece of land, and yet another and another.

We All Have a Diamond, a Divine Nature Inside Us

We can learn from this story that there are diamonds right beneath our feet; we will find diamonds right in our backyard or in our flower gardens. There may be different opinions about how good a parable this story is. But there is a reason why this story became so legendary. It is because there is a universal message within it that touched people's minds.

All of us have divine nature within us, because we are all children of God. This is absolutely true. If we dig deep enough within us, each of us will find the nature of God hidden inside. Very sadly, so many of us give up too early. Like the farmer who gave up three inches above the diamond layer, many of us think that it will be impossible to find any diamonds in such a desolate land. We believe that there are talented and capable people out there who are loved by God but that it can never be ourselves. Somehow, we come to believe that we are nobodies, that we were born as nobodies, and that we have always been treated as nobodies. We have neither an impressive résumé, nor experiences, nor income, so we come to believe that we are not capable of greatness.

But at heart, the moral of the story of the diamond miners is that all of us who believe that we are not capable of anything extraordinary are absolutely wrong. This story became so widespread and was told countless times because it is a Truth that we are all children of God. This is what I am always teaching at Happy Science. There are diamonds lying within everyone, and every one of us will be able to uncover them as long as we keep digging just a little further. This story warns us of our tendency to believe that chances will come to others but not to us, and we must learn from it.

· 3 ·

WE BECOME WHAT WE ARE ALWAYS THINKING ABOUT

• ─────────────────────────────── •

Reasons Why Our Dreams Do Not Come True

I often say that we humans are what we are always thinking about—that who you think you are is what creates
your future. Many people come to me and say, "I have
been thinking about my dreams forever, but they have
not come true yet. Can dreams really come true just by
thinking about them?" The story about the two diamond
miners may give us hints to the answer to this question. But
I will share another story with you.

In the United States, "the laws of success" became
very popular in the latter part of the nineteenth century
and into the twentieth century, when the nation flour-
ished. The concept that you can change yourself by
changing the way you think became popular in fields
such as psychology. One day, an office worker asked
someone who preached this philosophy, "You say that
people will become what they are always thinking about.
I have always dreamed of quitting being an office worker,

becoming a successful businessman, and being very wealthy. But I am still an average office worker. What am I doing wrong?"

The speaker said, "Take a good look at yourself in the mirror. Anyone who looks at you will see that you are an office worker, don't you think? If you really want to stop being an office worker and become a successful salesman or an entrepreneur, you have to start with your appearance. You have to reflect on the outside what you are thinking about on the inside. It is not enough just to think about it inside your mind. If you are really thinking about it, then it should become externalized in your attitude and your physical appearance. You need to show it to everyone so they can see what you are thinking about. Take a look yourself, and you will realize that you look like an office worker."

The office worker agreed. The speaker advised him to begin by getting a new necktie and a brand new suit so he could start dressing like a successful entrepreneur. The moral of the story is that if our thoughts change, then our external appearance should also change as a result of our thoughts.

Show What You Are Thinking About in Your Attitude and Appearance

Even if you are the president of a country, if you wear a garbage collector's uniform and stand near a garbage truck, no one will think that you are the president. This applies to all of us. Whoever you are or are trying to be, you need to dress the part and have the appropriate image. Whatever is in your heart and mind needs to be expressed in your attitude and your actions. It should be expressed in the way you carry yourself and present yourself to others. Many people do not realize the importance of expressing what is inside on the outside.

This is the effort that we need to put in, the extra three inches that we need to dig before we hit the diamond layer in the earth. Do not be like the office worker who dreamed of becoming successful but forgot to take the first step toward his dream. While your life is determined by what you are always thinking about, your thoughts cannot be just vague ideas. If you are really thinking about your dream, you should express it by taking steps toward actualizing it. We should express our thoughts visibly in our attitude. We should use our words to speak our thoughts aloud. We should take action based on our thoughts. And our thoughts should be represented in our physical appearance. Never be afraid to express your thoughts outwardly in every possible way.

· **4** ·

KNOWLEDGE IS POWER

Make the Effort to Know
Twice or Thrice As Much As Others Know

The way we think is a crucial part of our lives. It is absolutely true that we become the person that we think we are. This is something I learned deeply as a child by suffering from a horrible inferiority complex. In my journey to overcome it, I started by learning that we cannot change our lives for the positive unless we change our way of thinking. And one of the first things my experience taught me was that knowledge is power. The Western philosopher Francis Bacon is known for this quote. It means that to have knowledge of something can give us power. And I believe that the original meaning of the word "knowledge" described not simple information, but God's grace. For instance, the divine messages that we receive from God as His grace are an example of the kind of knowledge that Bacon was referring to. But I believe that we can also include information as part of the meaning of "knowledge."

I encountered this phrase, "knowledge is power,"

when I was in college, and looking back, I am convinced that these words were a profound truth. It is absolutely the truth that knowledge gives us power. So many people make judgments based on how intelligent people were when they were young. Many of us judge ourselves based on these same standards. But I discovered that whether you are a bright person or not, you will reap results as long as you have knowledge. Whether you know something because you are naturally bright or because you studied it, the outcome will be the same. When I look at results, I see no differences between these two types of people.

I cannot stress enough how true this saying is, that knowledge is power. If someone who is not so bright studies enough to gain twice or three times the knowledge of someone who is considered very bright in that subject or field, the former person will be able to accomplish much more than the latter. This is the moral of the phrase "knowledge is power," and I learned the profoundness of this truth through my own experiences.

I Started by Reading Many Books

When I think back to my college years attending the University of Tokyo, I am reminded of having felt inferior to all the smart people that surrounded me. The country bumpkin that I was assumed that the other students were all natural born geniuses. But when I learned about the powerful principle that "knowledge is power," I started to see the possibility of catching up to them or even outrunning them, as long as I had the necessary knowledge. This was when I decided to stop wasting time thinking about whether or not I was intelligent and to start studying and gaining knowledge instead.

So I began reading many books. I decided to read more books than any of my naturally bright peers, and I read as many books as I possibly could. The tables turned as my knowledge increased. In a debate, someone without knowledge cannot win against someone with knowledge. Someone who is naturally intelligent will be able to give good arguments even when they only have to discuss their own opinions, but they do not stand a chance against someone who possesses a lot of knowledge and has studied well.

If you keep studying and aim to gain two to three times more knowledge than others have, you will achieve more compared with people whom you think were born with natural intelligence. You will be amazed at how true this is and what you can achieve through genuine discipline and effort.

Many of us make the mistake of believing that what makes us intelligent is quick mastery of important points. But the truth is that knowledge is what gives us true power.

· 5 ·

TIME IS MONEY
AND MONEY IS TIME

Everyone Has an Equal Amount of Time Per Day

The next truth that I discovered and developed a deep understanding of was a famous quote from Benjamin Franklin found in his *Poor Richard's Almanac*: "Time is money."

All of us are given twenty-four hours in a day, and most of us live a total of about twenty thousand days. No matter who we are, we can never change this fact. We are all equal in the amount of time we are given in our lives. Whether or not we become successful, we are given no more and no less than twenty-four hours in a day, and we are given this time to use freely for our success or for our failure. It is not as though the successful have one hundred hours in a day and the unsuccessful only twenty-four.

Consequently, if there is such a thing as equality, it is not equality of ability but equality of time. There is perfect equality in the number of hours each of us are given in a day. I learned that whether we achieve greatness or not, each of us lives for seven or eight decades, and what we achieve depends on how we use the time we are given each day and throughout our lives.

I think that this is a lesson you can integrate into your life quite easily when you are young, but it is something that can be applied to businesspeople, too. Some people use their twenty-four hours a day to become CEOs, while others use them to keep working as office workers.

God will never shout to us from Heaven about how we should use our time. We are not going to hear God telling us to stop wasting our time and encouraging us to work harder and study harder. God simply provides us twenty-four hours every day, no less. He never suddenly changes it to twelve hours or five hours. And it is our task to find the best way to use our time.

In the final analysis, life is a continual process of defining and redefining the ways we use the twenty-four hours in each of our days. When we master how we use our time, we can become victorious in our lives. So take control of your time, and think about what you should do to produce as many positive things as possible.

You Need Perseverance to Achieve Success

There is another valuable factor in achieving success,

and that is perseverance. Even someone with outstanding abilities will not achieve success if perseverance is lacking. Gambling is probably the only possible way of making a lot of money in just twenty-four hours. But of course, you will never earn an ongoing income by gambling at casinos, horse races, bike races, or by buying lottery tickets.

I have found that most people who are not successful need to have more perseverance. Many of us will meet many people through life who are bright and talented and were blessed by fortunate circumstances but who ironically have not achieved much in life. This occurs because they did not possess strong persistence and the ability to endure through time.

Intelligent people tend to give up easily, simply because they are too quick to make judgments. It is a shame that they do not use their intelligence to make good judgments, for often they make the wrong premature judgment. As with the diamond miner, success will always evade us as long as we keep giving up and moving on to the next spot of land, believing that we will find the diamond layer more quickly by digging somewhere else. For example, some of us who are intelligent might find many sources of dissatisfaction at work and so might keep changing jobs. However, if we stick with one job for a little while longer, we might become experts. So many of us give up just inches before that opportunity comes, simply because we did not have enough per-severance. In some cases, we will get angry at people around us because we blame them for our own inability to succeed. This often leads people with talent and ability away from success.

We need to be able to control and master our minds. And if we find this difficult, we need to realize that we are lacking an important virtue. I hope that everyone will understand and discover the value in the truth, "Time is money." This was one of the very small forms of enlighten-ment that I achieved during my younger years.

Wealth Can Save Time

I describe another truth that I learned as a college stu-dent as, "Money is time." The words are reversed from the previous saying, "Time is money." It conveys the truth that a certain amount of money can buy you time. Money can effectively help you use time more efficiently and may even speed up your success.

This truth is absolutely valuable knowledge for an entrepreneur. Concentration of wealth is the essence of the principle of capitalism. One thousand dollars may not accomplish much if many people use one thousand dollars separately for different things. But if we combine that money into one large sum of several million, tens of millions, or hundreds of millions of dollars, imagine what we can achieve. Through concentrating wealth for a common cause, we can accomplish bigger feats and create new things of value. This is what capitalism is essentially about, described in the simplest terms.

I have often criticized communist ideology because communist notions of equality are based on a division and distribution of wealth for the purpose of equalization. For example, the current administration under the Democratic Party of Japan will probably resort to monetary handouts of the same amount of money to all the victims of the Great East Japan Earthquake. It is not difficult to guess that they will implement a policy along those lines, because that is how a socialist government thinks. The problem with this way of thinking is that the distribution of wealth in such a manner never creates any additional value beyond what is handed out. On the other hand, if that same amount of money were concentrated and used for the right purpose, it could accomplish something much greater. This was the reason why countries who adhered to democracy and capitalism achieved development.

This applies to individuals, too. The people who have not achieved much success in life are those who lack a deep awareness of this truth and instead adhere to a communist philosophy. It is unfortunate to see many people fall into this trap. For example, you will be able to buy more books with a larger income. With more money, you will also be able to buy a large enough house to store all your books. Money can also help you travel faster by enabling you to purchase a car, use the bullet train, or travel by plane.

When I was a student, I used to take the ferry from the Chiba Harbor to my hometown in Tokushima Prefecture. The tickets for the bullet train were very expensive back then. The ferry cost less than half as much—it was perhaps a quarter of the price of the bullet train. It took twenty-four hours to get from Chiba to Tokushima by ferry, so I would often spend the journey lying about and reading books. I was able to afford the bullet train only much later and I never took a plane home during college. Some of my friends bought plane tickets with a student discount, but it was still too expensive for my budget. So it is a very important lesson to learn that wealth is very effective in saving us time.

· 6 ·

USE SUBDIVISION TO TACKLE DIFFICULT PROBLEMS

⸺

No Wild Boars Are Bigger than the Mountain

The last important point for a young person's path to success is to be mindful that when we are young, our problems tend to appear much bigger than they actually are. The difficulties and problems we face can feel like a mountain too large to climb, so many young people give up.

If you ever encounter a situation like this, remember the proverb that says, "No wild boar is ever bigger than the mountain." No matter how large a boar a frightened hunter encounters, it can never be larger than the mountain. This proverb is meant to help people who become scared for little reason and are unable to succeed because their irrational fears drive them to run away from their problems.

We can also break down our most difficult problems into smaller components that will be easier to solve. If we tackle the smaller problems one by one, we will build a path to overcome them. For example, say there is a bridge that has a maximum load of five tons. On a daily basis, though, the total weight of the countless vehicles that use the bridge is probably hundreds or even thousands of tons. So even though this bridge may be able to support five tons at any given time, it is supporting a much heavier load every day.

It is the same with life. If we take on problems that weigh hundreds or thousands of tons all at once, the weight of our problems will crush us. But we can handle all those problems if we carry them in smaller loads, one by one over time.

Those Who Do Not Give Up Will Succeed

Remember that you cannot solve all your problems at once. We become distressed, give up, and even commit suicide, because we try to solve all our problems in one day. Instead, if you divide your problems into portions that you can handle each day and solve them one by one, you will be able to make progress little by little and eventually solve even the most difficult of problems.

When we think that we are not very smart, for instance, and worry about how much effort we will need to put into our studies to achieve good grades, we may be daunted by the sheer amount that we need to learn and believe that it is an impossible feat. But if we use this principle of dividing and conquering, doing a little every day, we will reach our goal some day. It may take us three years or five years to learn what others spend one year on. But no matter how long it takes, we will reach our goal, and those who do not give up on the way are those who succeed.

Even if you are intelligent, you will not become successful if you give up. On the other hand, even if you are not considered to be the most intelligent, as long as you persist, persevere, and use the principle of dividing and conquering every day, I assure you that you will be on the path to success. I can promise you that. I hope that my teachings and examples of the way to success will be useful to many of you.

5

MAGNIFYING YOUR COURAGE A HUNDREDFOLD

· 1 ·

FIND YOUR CALLING

●————————————————————————●

Courage Is One of the Perks of Youth

In this chapter I would like to share a way that anyone can empower themselves with enormous courage. Mustering courage was the first big task I faced in starting Happy Science, back in 1986. If I had not had the courage to found a new religious organization, Happy Science would never have existed; courage was the first deciding factor.

I wrote in my book *Be Brave** that many people who are studious have a tendency to lose courage. This book was compiled from answers I had given to questions from people who had been students just one or two years previously. The truth is that I used to be one of these studious people who was tempted to take the route that seemed more advantageous—the one that would be most publicly acceptable and give me the least trouble. I know from my own experience how difficult it is to set aside our desire for recognition and instead decide to use passion

---

* Happy Science published *Be Brave* internally, for its members.

and will to achieve something very valuable.

However, courage is one of the perks of youth. As we grow older and turn forty, fifty, or sixty, we become increasingly burdened by things that we cannot abandon, such as our family, company, social status, reputation, and property. But those of you who are in your late teens or early twenties should have very few things weighing you down. Your hearts are pure and filled with hope for the future.

The First Step to Courage Is Making the Decision to Fulfill Your Mission

Ever since I founded Happy Science, I have made progress through sure-footed steps, one step at a time. Life is a constant struggle. We can never accomplish anything unless someone stands up and acts with courage. No matter what we are aiming to do, we will always be faced with resistance in the beginning.

Today Happy Science has many followers, but when I first attained spiritual awareness, there was no one to support me. Even my family had difficulty believing in me. To be honest, I also doubted myself. All through my twenties, I struggled painfully to believe that such an extraordinary calling could be my mission in life.

I had just finished studying undergraduate law at the

University of Tokyo and had begun a career at a major trading company. I was sent to the New York office and was considered to be an exceptional employee—the kind that comes along only once in a decade. Meanwhile, in stark contrast to the secular side of my life, many holy spirits who professed to come from the higher parts of Heaven began to visit me with their messages. And finally, one day, they said to me, "Believe in our words. Rise to your feet, and begin your mission alone." If you had been me, would you have believed them? Would you have thrown away the promising future that was guaranteed to you and started something completely on your own?

At the age of thirty, I made the decision to quit my job and follow my calling with no income at all. I did this because I realized that my calling was everything to my life, regardless of whether anyone ever believes in me. As I wrote in *Be Brave*, courage starts with making the decision to fulfill your mission, your duty to the world. You must find your calling, and when you are sure that it is your mission in life, take the first brave step of following your calling, of fulfilling your duty to the world.

The Enlightenment of Young Adulthood

The world is full of unique people, each with their own path through life, unique talents and abilities, strengths and weaknesses, and likes and dislikes. If you discover a passionate voice from deep within you rising over and over, this must be your calling and your mission in life.

The seed that will some day blossom into your mission was planted within you long ago. We begin our journey to discovering our calling beginning at the age of twenty and continuing through our early adulthood. It is one of the goals at this stage of our life to find out, as part of our enlightenment, what purpose we were born for, what we want to accomplish in life, and how we want to end our lives. Each of us needs to ask ourselves these questions and search for the answers.

So first and foremost, you must take a long, hard look at who you are. Reflect on your talents and abilities, your personality, your character traits, your life over the last twenty years, and the way you have lived thus far. Use this contemplation to try to find your mission and calling. This will become your first enlightenment in life.

Enlightenment is necessary for all people, from all walks of life. Some of us may have the misconception that only religious people attain enlightenment, but this is not true. Enlightenment is necessary and possible for all of us on our unique journeys. So what makes someone an enlightened person? An enlightened person is someone who has become awakened.

So I say to you all: "Be awakened! Become an awakened person!" If you find that scales have covered your eyes, peel the scales off and look at the world through your real eyes. Do not let the norms of society and the opinions of other adults cloud your view. Use your own real eyes to discover what you should make of yourself in life. This self-discovery is what makes an awakened person, and it is a valuable enlightenment of young adulthood. It is the first step on our path to even higher enlightenment.

· 2 ·

TAKE ON CHALLENGES AND DO NOT FEAR FAILURE

Do Not Seek a Life Without Setbacks and Failures

In the course of our lives, we will come upon many unexpected paths and travel many different roads. As we travel down these paths and roads, we should never seek a life without setbacks and failures. You should never, not even for a millisecond, aim for a life of total success, free from all mistakes, setbacks, adversities, and struggles. Appreciate your youth; do not be like some older people who have lived their entire lives trying to avoid failure. If you are young, then keep challenging yourself. Keep taking on new and difficult challenges. Take hold of what you have to do, even if it challenges the established norms of society. Keep trying. What matters is that we never give up.

Do not be afraid of failure. The greatest obstacle to taking brave action is the fear of failure. But the only thing we should be afraid of is fear itself. Be wary of any fears and insecurities that could be lurking in your mind, and fight them with all your might. Most of our fears and worries are simply the result of our inexperience and of not knowing what lies ahead of us.

How To Conquer Our Fears

There is one sure-fire way to conquer our fears, and that is to challenge ourselves to do what we are most afraid of. Our fears will vanish the moment we face them and decide to fight them. It does not matter whether we fail or succeed in that challenge. For I will guarantee you that the moment we face our fears, the substance of that fear will disappear, and we will be left with only valuable experiences.

One of these experiences is that we will have conquered our fear. A second experience that we reap is the crushed feeling of being unsuccessful at a colossal challenge, in spite of having given it everything we had— every drop of wisdom, all our strength, and our fighting spirit. Even if we fail at our challenge, this experience will never be negative. It is the crushing feeling that we often experience in our younger years, the indescribable feeling of inconsolable wretchedness, that miserable feeling, and our self-reproach for our ignorance, that will become a perpetual driving force through the many battles we will face in later decades.

These crushed feelings will give us the thirst for growth that propels us forward. Conquering these feelings through countless failures will gradually help us mature into adulthood. One day, you will think back to your twenties, and the mistakes you made then will appear small. You will see them as meaningful experiences that provided valuable lessons, and at that point, you will know that you have grown and fully matured. This is when you will be ready to lead the people that come after you to the right path, and for this purpose, you should tackle as many challenges as you can.

· 3 ·

AIM TO BECOME A PROFESSIONAL

●————————————————————————●

We Become Professionals by Giving Everything We Have, Every Day

Ever since I founded Happy Science, I have continuously challenged myself and have constantly faced new challenges that I had no experience with. One example is my lectures. I gave my first lecture on November 23, 1986, to a small audience of ninety people. Then, on March 8, 1987, I gave a public lecture called "The Principle of Happiness" at the Ushigome Public Hall in front of four hundred people. This was followed by my second public lecture called "The Principle of Love" held on May 31 of the same year at Chiyoda Public Hall, this time for an audience of one thousand. Since then, the crowds have kept growing. A year later, in 1988, I gave another lecture at Hibiya Public Hall, a venue that holds two thousand people. And in 1989, I delivered another one, at the Ryogoku Sumo Hall, that attracted 8,500 people. The next year, in 1990, I gave several lectures at the Makuhari Messe International Convention Complex in Chiba Prefecture; these lectures attracted between twelve thousand and eighteen thousand people. In 1991, I held a lecture* at Tokyo Dome for fifty thousand people. Later, I gave lectures at Tokyo Dome that were broadcast live all over the country.

I was still in my early thirties in 1991, when I gave my first lecture at Tokyo Dome. Time flew by, and within just a few years of its founding, Happy Science grew into a giant organization. When I ask myself how I achieved this, it is easy to see the answer. My success came from giving every lecture everything that I had, every single time. By giving this series of intensely earnest lectures, I became the professional that I am today.

You will be pursuing careers in various fields, and I am sure that many of the questions you have in mind are about choosing the right career. I can hear the voices of your hearts, wondering how you should live your lives, what kinds of jobs you will be successful in, and what you should do to perform well in your jobs.

There is only one answer to these questions: Give it everything you've got. You will become a professional in any career as long as you continue to give your best each and every day. The sum of each day's efforts will lead you to your goal, no matter what job you choose.

But what does it mean to give it everything you've got? This is not about practicing your swing at the Japa-

---

* This lecture was held to celebrate Ryuho Okawa's birthday.

nese fencing school. You are fighting a duel with real swords that can cut you. Anyone who survives this world of real duels will grow into a professional. This is true without exception, no matter what walk of life you choose.

Professionals Gracefully Accept and Conquer Adversity

Today the world is facing a huge international recession. In 2009, some people claimed that we were in the worst financial crisis in a hundred years. Others claim that we are going through another great depression. I do not agree. These are just excuses intended to attract the sympathy of the people and the help of governments.

If you are a true professional, you must fight. If you are a true professional entrepreneur, fight this adversity with courage. If you are a professional businessman, no matter how large the crisis, face it with your resourcefulness, work as hard as you can, and tackle it with fervor. It is impossible for every business around the globe to go bankrupt. The businesses that go under are those with weak and irresponsible management. If you are the CEO of a business, it is your responsibility to save your company. But even if you are a brand new employee, you should accept this adversity with grace and do your best to help your company out of the crisis. We must all face our adversity and conquer it.

The economy will always go through ups and downs. We should never fall into the delusion that times will always be favorable to us or that our business's rapid growth will continue forever. Economic downturns occur all the time and are easily predictable. Smaller ones happen every three years to ten years. The bigger recessions arrive every several decades. So as professionals, we should make the effort every day to be prepared to overcome any difficulties or struggles that we may face down the road. This is the way to be a professional.

Resolve to Take On Greater Responsibilities

A true professional bears many heavy responsibilities. The weight of the responsibilities you bear is a measure of what kind of professional you are. In your development, you will be able to grow as far as your range of responsibilities will allow. We should make the effort every day, year after year, to be able to bear heavier responsibilities.

Always remember that the size of the responsibilities that a person can bear is a measure of that person's stature. Those of us who continue to challenge ourselves with new things are also those who are trying to take on bigger responsibilities. What is most important is that we always face new challenges, attempt things that no one has done before, and do what's right, even if people try to stop us.

What makes us professionals is that we are always giving each day everything that we have and that we are resolved to take on ever-greater responsibilities. This is about having the attitude of taking risks. Those who avoid taking risks will not achieve big successes, nor will they be respected by others. So jump headlong into those risks, and you will see yourself continue to grow into a greater human being.

· 4 ·

YOU CAN MAKE YOUR COURAGE A HUNDRED TIMES STRONGER

Be Proactive and Always Look For Ways to Make It Happen

You will face many situations in life that will feel impossible to overcome, especially those of you who are younger. I have been through this, too. When we find ourselves in adversity, we should not offer a list of reasons to persuade everyone why our situation is impossible to overcome. Even if a problem seems insurmountable, take a step back. Take a close look, and search for a solution. Search for a way to overcome the problem, and break through it.

This is what it means to be positive. Always try to see things in a constructive light. Look for a way to solve the problem, a way to break through it, a way to overcome adversity, and create a new path, a solution that we have not thought of yet—a new idea. Thinking of reasons why we cannot do something should be our last resort. Instead you should think about how to make things happen, especially if you are young. This is what I always do.

When I start a new project, I am often faced with resistance. People often tell me that it is impossible to succeed because we have never done anything like it before. I have made it my policy to try to do things that everyone opposes, because those are the ideas that have a greater chance of success. If many people believe that a project will be unsuccessful, very few people will attempt it. This is why I have taken on board many ideas that people have deemed impossible, too challenging, and too difficult.

For example, I had to be brave to open Happy Science branches throughout Japan and abroad, and I am planning to establish more throughout the world. I also needed courage to start Happy Science Academy in Tochigi Prefecture and Shiga Prefecture and to open Happy Science University in 2015. My aspiration of establishing the Happiness Realization Party, our political party, was also realized in 2009. This had been a goal of mine since I founded Happy Science in 1989.

Both Religion and Politics Exist to Promote People's Happiness

It is true that religions mainly serve in the spiritual field of leading souls to salvation and offering spiritual guidance. But there are two sides to happiness. One side is the happiness that we gain in finding salvation for our souls, finding solace, and attaining peace of mind. The other side is the happiness that is found in receiving help with the difficulties and hardships that we grapple with in our everyday lives in this world. Both religion and government have roles to play in providing this latter form of happiness.

If the government becomes too weak, then religion needs to stand up. Still, there are limitations to what a religion can accomplish. Religions cannot pass new laws or create and implement new policies. Unfortunately, religion cannot fully reach out to people who need real help getting through their daily lives.

Religion has traditionally served three major purposes: saving people from poverty and disease and ending conflicts. But political power is also necessary in tackling these issues. Part of the purpose of politicians, judges, lawyers, prosecutors, and lawmakers is to decrease poverty, help the sick, and end conflicts. Therefore, religion and politics cannot be completely separated from each other. Each approaches these issues from a different angle, but they share the common goal of making people happier. They should unite, not polarize, their strength and cooperate to create a better nation and a better world.

There Is No Prosperity For a Country That Does Not Respect Religious Leaders and Politicians

Six decades after World War II, Japan has become a very prosperous country, but there is something important that we need to think about. The prosperity of a country that does not respect religions and religious leaders who are worthy of respect will not last long. There are religious leaders who are devoting themselves to the holy duties of attuning their minds to the will of God and guiding people to salvation. Unfortunately, religious leaders have been scorned and devalued in Japan since the end of World War II. This has to stop.

If this state of things continues, then Japan's prosperity will be a bubble that will inevitably burst. We cannot achieve prosperity if we lose sight of the right path and end up chasing after worldly goals. A country that does not respect its religious leaders will not be able to flourish forever.

A country that does not respect its politicians will not flourish either. The Japanese media is filled with articles and reports that demean, ridicule, and criticize our politicians as if it is their right to do so. Our politicians have practically become a laughingstock. If the political leaders of this country are lowly and greedy, have an ignoble character, and are working only for their own interests, it should be an embarrassment to have elected them as our leaders. At the least, it has deeply embarrassed me. Politicians should be leaders worthy of our respect who aim to lead the nation with high aspirations. There should never be a nation where people do not respect their politicians.

I believe that the time has arrived for all of us to mend our ways and elect leaders who are worthy of our respect. We must set out once and for all to create a government and political system that can do the right things. In 2009, there was a leadership change from the Liberal Democratic Party to the Democratic Party of Japan, both of which are major political parties in Japan. But I did not see the kind of politics that were worthy of our respect in the new administration.

When We Awaken to Our Mission and Ideals, Our Courage Will Increase a Hundredfold

Please never have the kind of mindset that puts down, scorns, minimizes, or abases religion and politics. Please never express thoughts like these. There are religious leaders and politicians who are working earnestly to make the world a better place, and these people are professionals who are worthy of their place.

I am counting on the brave decisions and actions of those in the younger generations. What is most valuable for our world is to create a prosperity that comes from our courage, resolution, and action. With these ingredients, we can create the future of our dreams.

The political activities of the Happiness Realization Party are one of the tools that I use to further its goal of improving the world. I believe that the work of our political party is necessary for this endeavor. In time, I hope that our party will expand abroad and create an extraordinary political movement throughout the world. I hope that the youth of today will be brave. Embrace the passion of a devoted religious missionary, join the movement to improve politics, and help bring our ideals into reality.

Your physical stamina may not power up a hundredfold. Your intelligence may not improve by a hundredfold. The length of your life may not extend a hundredfold. But I promise you that you can make your courage a hundred times stronger than it is now. I assure you that when we awaken to our true mission and ideals, our courage will grow tremendously.

It is my deepest hope that all of us will face our adversities and hardships with our courage a hundred times stronger. I assure you that the path will open for you. Please never become a cowardly cynic who ridicules and scorns others and talks behind people's back. Please be brave and aspire to take responsibility for the world. This is my message to everyone.

AFTERWORD

In anything we do, the most important thing is to take the first step. The second important thing is to keep going, and keep using creativity and originality.

There is no telling how many times I have been saved by the phrase "Think big!" I began using this phrase during my "boot camp" training in the United States, and it might have been the most important enlightenment of my younger years.

"Be positive!" and "Be brave!" are phrases that I would pair with "Think Big!" I hope that many of the world's young people will read this book about my philosophy of success.

Ryuho Okawa
Founder and CEO
Happy Science Group
February 14, 2012

The contents of this book were compiled from the following lectures:

CHAPTER 1
Building a Bright Future
[Mirai Kaitaku Hō]
April 19, 2008 at Tokyo Shoshinkan, Tokyo

CHAPTER 2
Aim to Achieve Success Gracefully!
[Sawayakana Seikō O!]
May 3, 2008 at Tokyo Shoshinkan, Tokyo

CHAPTER 3
Think Big!
[Think Big!]
August 1, 2010 at Hakone Shoja, Kanagawa

CHAPTER 4
The Way to Success
[Seikō E No Michi]
April 29, 2011 at Tokyo Shoshinkan, Tokyo

CHAPTER 5
Magnifying Your Courage a Hundredfold
[Yūki Hyakubai Hō]
May 10, 2009 at The Tokyo Metropolitan Hibiya Public Hall, Tokyo

About the Author

RYUHO OKAWA is a global visionary, renowned spiritual leader, and best-selling author in Japan with a simple goal: to help people find true happiness and create a better world.

His deep compassion and sense of responsibility for the happiness of each individual has prompted him to publish over 2,000 titles of religious, spiritual, and self-development teachings, covering a broad range of topics including how our thoughts influence reality, the nature of love, and the path to enlightenment. He also writes on the topics of management and economy, as well as the relationship between religion and politics in the global context. To date, Okawa's books have sold over 100 million copies worldwide and been translated into 28 languages.

Okawa has dedicated himself to improving society and creating a better world. In 1986, Okawa founded Happy Science as a spiritual movement dedicated to bringing greater happiness to humankind by uniting religions and cultures to live in harmony. Happy Science has grown rapidly from its beginnings in Japan to a worldwide organization with over 10 million members. Okawa is compassionately committed to the spiritual growth of others. In addition to writing and publishing books, he continues to give lectures around the world.

About Happy Science

Happy Science is a global movement that empowers individuals to find purpose and spiritual happiness and to share that happiness with their families, societies, and the world. With more than twelve million members around the world, Happy Science aims to increase awareness of spiritual truths and expand our capacity for love, compassion, and joy so that together we can create the kind of world we all wish to live in.

Activities at Happy Science are based on the Principles of Happiness (Love, Wisdom, Self-Reflection, and Progress). These principles embrace worldwide philosophies and beliefs, transcending boundaries of culture and religions.

Love teaches us to give ourselves freely without expecting anything in return; it encompasses giving, nurturing, and forgiveness.

Wisdom leads us to the insights of spiritual truths, and opens us to the true meaning of life and the will of God (the universe, the highest power, Buddha).

Self-Reflection brings a mindful, nonjudgmental lens to our thoughts and actions to help us find our truest selves—the essence of our souls—and deepen our connection to the highest power. It helps us attain a clean and peaceful mind and leads us to the right life path.

Progress emphasizes the positive, dynamic aspects of our spiritual growth—actions we can take to manifest and spread happiness around the world. It's a path that not only expands our soul growth, but also furthers the collective potential of the world we live in.

Programs and Events

The doors of Happy Science are open to all. We offer a variety of programs and events, including self-exploration and self-growth programs, spiritual seminars, meditation and contemplation sessions, study groups, and book events.

Our programs are designed to:

- Deepen your understanding of your purpose and meaning in life
- Improve your relationships and increase your capacity to love unconditionally
- Attain a peace of mind, decrease anxiety and stress, and feel positive
- Gain deeper insights and broader perspective on the world
- Learn how to overcome life's challenges
  ... and much more.

For more information, visit our website at happyscience-na.org or happy-science.org.

International Seminars

Each year, friends from all over the world join our international seminars, held at our faith centers in Japan. Different programs are offered each year and cover a wide variety of topics, including improving relationships, practicing the Eightfold Path to enlightenment, and loving yourself, to name just a few.

Happy Science Monthly

Our monthly publication covers the latest featured lectures, members' life-changing experiences and other news from members around the world, book reviews, and many other topics. Downloadable PDF files are available at happyscience-na.org. Copies and back issues in Portuguese, Chinese, and other languages are available upon request. For more information, contact us via e-mail at tokyo@happy-science.org.

Contact Information

Happy Science is a worldwide organization with faith centers around the globe. For a comprehensive list of centers, visit the worldwide directory at happy-science.org or happyscience-na.org. The following are some of the many Happy Science locations:

United States and Canada

New York
79 Franklin Street
New York, NY 10013
Phone: 212-343-7972
Fax: 212-343-7973
Email: ny@happy-science.org
website: newyork.happyscience-na.org

Los Angeles
1590 E. Del Mar Blvd.
Pasadena, CA 91106
Phone: 626-395-7775
Fax: 626-395-7776
Email: la@happy-science.org
website: losangeles.happyscience-na.org

Orange County
10231 Slater Ave #204
Fountain Valley, CA 92708
Phone: 714-745-1140
Email: oc@happy-science.org

San Diego
Email: sandiego@happy-science.org

San Francisco
525 Clinton Street
Redwood City, CA 94062
Phone/Fax: 650-363-2777
Email: sf@happy-science.org
website: sanfrancisco.happyscience-na.org

Florida
5208 8th St, Zephyrhills,
FL 33542, USA
Phone: 813-715-0000
Fax: 813-715-0010
Email: florida@happy-science.org
website: florida.happyscience-na.org

New Jersey
725 River Rd. #102B
Edgewater, NJ 07025
Phone: 201-313-0127
Fax: 201-313-0120
Email: nj@happy-science.org
website: newjersey.happyscience-na.org

Atlanta
1874 Piedmont Ave. NE
Suite 360-C
Atlanta, GA 30324
Phone: 404-892-7770
Email: atlanta@happy-science.org
website: atlanta.happyscience-na.org

Hawaii
1221 Kapiolani Blvd., Suite 920
Honolulu, HI 96814
Phone: 808-591-9772
Fax: 808-591-9776
Email: hi@happy-science.org
website: hawaii.happyscience-na.org

Kauai
4504 Kukui Street
Dragon Building Suite 21
Kapaa, HI 96746
Phone: 808-822-7007
Fax: 808-822-6007
Email: kauai-hi@happy-science.org
website: happyscience-kauai.org

Toronto
323 College Street,
Toronto, ON M5T 1S2
Canada
Phone/Fax: 1-416-901-3747
Email: toronto@happy-science.org
website: happyscience-na.org

Vancouver
#212-2609 East 49th Avenue
Vancouver, V5S 1J9
Canada
Phone: 1-604-437-7735
Fax: 1-604-437-7764
Email: vancouver@happy-science.org
website: happyscience-na.org

INTERNATIONAL

Tokyo
1-6-7 Togoshi
Shinagawa, Tokyo, 142-0041
Japan
Phone: 81-3-6384-5770
Fax: 81-3-6384-5776
Email: tokyo@happy-science.org
website: happy-science.org

London
3 Margaret Street,
London, W1W 8RE
United Kingdom
Phone: 44-20-7323-9255
Fax: 44-20-7323-9344
Email: eu@happy-science.org
website: happyscience-uk.org

Sydney
516 Pacific Hwy
Lane Cove North,
2066 NSW
Australia
Phone: 61-2-9411-2877
Fax: 61-2-9411-2822
Email: aus@happy-science.org
website: happyscience.org.au

Brazil Headquarters
Rua. Domingos de Morais 1154,
Vila Mariana, Sao Paulo,
CEP 04009-002
Brazil
Phone: 55-11-5088-3800
Fax: 55-11-5088-3806
Email: sp@happy-science.org
website: cienciadafelicidade.com.br

Jundiai
Rua Congo, 447,
Jd.Bonfiglioli, Jundiai- CEP
13207 - 340
Phone: 55-11-4587-5952
Email: jundiai@happy-sciece.org

Seoul
74, Sadang-ro 27-gil,
Dongjak-gu, Seoul, Korea
Phone: 82-2-3478-8777
Fax: 82-2-3478-9777
Email: korea@happy-science.org
website: happyscience-korea.org

Taipei
No. 89, Lane 155, Dunhua N. Road
Songshan District
Taipei City 105
Taiwan
Phone: 886-2-2719-9377
Fax: 886-2-2719-5570
Email: taiwan@happy-science.org
website: happyscience-tw.org

Malaysia
No 22A, Block2, Jalil Link
Jalan Jalil Jaya 2, Bukit Jalil
57000, Kuala Lumpur
Malaysia
Phone: 60-3-8998-7877
Fax: 60-3-8998-7977
Email: Malaysia@happy-science.org
Website: happyscience.org.my

Nepal
Kathmandu Metropolitan City,
Ward No. 15, Ring Road, Kimdol,
Sitapaila,Kathmandu
Nepal
Phone: 97-714-272931
Email: nepal@happy-science.org
nepaltrainingcenter@happy-science.org

Uganda
Plot 877 Rubaga Road Kampala
P.O. Box 34130
Kampala, Uganda
Phone: 256-79-3238-002
Email: uganda@happy-science.org

About IRH Press USA

IRH Press USA Inc. was founded in 2013 as an affiliated firm of IRH Press Co., Ltd. Based in New York, the press publishes books in various categories including spirituality, religion, and self-improvement, and publishes books by Ryuho Okawa, the author of 100 million books sold worldwide. For more information, visit OkawaBooks.com.

You can follow Ryuho Okawa and his latest book releases at <u>Goodreads</u>, <u>Facebook</u> and <u>Twitter</u>

Books by Ryuho Okawa

Find the keys to achieving happiness and success in our special calling

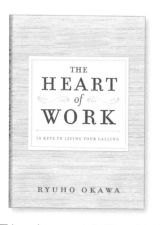

The Heart of Work

10 Keys to Living Your Calling

Success
Paperback · 5×7 · 224 pages
978-1-942125-03-7
US$12.95

There is so much fulfillment in discovering what we were meant to do and dedicating ourselves wholeheartedly to a job that we love doing. The goals we aspire to achieve through our lives and the ideals of who we want to become are vital to our success and happiness. In this book, Ryuho Okawa shares 10 key philosophies and goals to live by to guide us through our work lives and triumphantly live our calling. There are key principles that will help you get to the heart of work, manage your time well, prioritize your work, live with long health and vitality, achieve growth, and more. People of all walks of life—from the businessperson, executive, artist, teacher, mother, to even students—will find the keys to achieving happiness and success in our special calling.

Table of Contents

Your invitation to a more joyful, authentic life

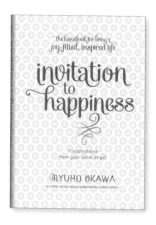

Invitation to Happiness

7 Inspirations
from Your Inner Angel

Self-Help
Hardcover · 5×7 · 176 pages
978-1-942125-01-3
US$16.99

Invitation to Happiness is a personal invitation and path to living a joy-filled, inspired life. It is the introduction to a spiritual journey guided by the driving force that guides us through life and the secret to living true to ourselves—our inner angel. We all have one, and each is our guide to spiritual happiness. The purpose of this book is to help the reader find joy by connecting with that inner voice, spirit, soul, or higher self.

Invitation to Happiness offers a new discovery of self and perspective. Through 7 inspirations, readers will be guided to find all the tools they need to live more confidently, peacefully, and authentically. The pages inside offer easy-to-use tools to get there, including practices for introspection, brief guided visualizations, tips and hints for contemplation, and even a discovery journal area to record inspirations from the inner angel. Through reading, contemplating and writing—readers will find simple step-by-step action plans that serve as a path to the truest self—allowing them to live a more confident, connected life of inner peace.

Music for inspiration

Free companion music is available for download at OkawaBooks.com. The readers can download 8 tracks of guided meditation to use along with the exercises in the book.

DOWNLOADABLE MUSIC AVAILABLE AT OKAWABOOKS.COM

▶ **Deep-Breathing Exercise**

▶ **Visualizing Your Dream**

▶ **Relationship Harmony**

...and more.

"Inside us all is a divine candle.
Spread that light to people around you and
help them light their own candles."

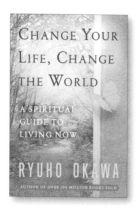

Change Your Life
Change the World

A Spiritual Guide to Living Now

Spirituality
Paperback · 5.8×8.8 · 192 pages
978-0-982698-50-1
US$16.95

Change Your Life, Change the World offers the timeless wisdom that has been inspiring millions of readers and followers around the world. In this book, Ryuho Okawa calls out to people of all nations to remember their true spiritual roots and accept that all of humanity, regardless of race, religion, or culture, was originally part of one gigantic family tree, called the Cosmic Tree. We are all responsive to the same creator, and are all part of a much larger universal family than we ever realized.

Change your Life, Change the World is a beacon of light, filled with universal lasting wisdom about the soul within each of us and the divine purpose of the human race within a vast universe. With this spiritual wisdom as our guide, each one of us has the power to change our lives and change the world.

What is the nature of the soul?
Where do we come from?

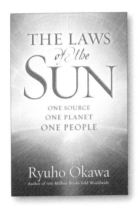

The Laws of the Sun

One Source, One Planet,
One People

Spirituality
Hardcover · 5.8×8.5 · 224 pages
978-1-937673-04-8
US$24.95

Imagine if you could ask God why He created this world and what spiritual laws He used to shape us—and everything around us. If we could understand His designs and intentions, we could discover what our goals in life should be and whether our actions move us closer to those goals or farther away. In these pages, we can see that God has been compassionately watching over humankind since the beginning of time, always sending envoys of His love in times of darkness. Once again, in a time of tremendous global instability, God's Truths are rising above the horizon and shining light onto the confusion we face today. They will inspire the world to appreciate that we all come from the same source, to let go of our differences, and to come together in peace and happiness: one people prospering on one planet. As we embrace the miracle that produced this book, we take the first steps to creating God's ultimate goal: Heaven on Earth.

If you could speak to Jesus, Buddha, Moses, or Muhammad, what would you ask?

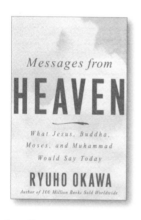

Messages from Heaven

What Jesus, Buddha, Muhammad, and Moses Would Say Today

Religion
Hardcover · 5.8×8.5 · 224 pages
978-1-941779-19-4
US$19.95

In **Messages from Heaven: What Jesus, Buddha, Moses, and Muhammad Would Say Today**, Ryuho Okawa shares the spiritual communication he had with these four spirits and the messages they want to share with people living today. This book offers spiritual wisdom and answers to the questions of the divine—messages of love, faith, miracles, gratitude, and forgiveness from Jesus; inquiries on humility, kindness, and enlightenment in the ordinary life with the Buddha; the meaning of righteousness, sin, and justice from Moses; and answers to questions about tolerance, faith, spirituality, and wealth from Muhammad. Through his conversations with four of the most influential religious leaders, Okawa explores the universal truths that thread between all faiths and offers insights to conquer our challenges that we face today. With this quest comes spiritual awakening as human souls, which unites each of us through the universal principles of love, wisdom, self-reflection, and progress.

This book is your gate to heaven.

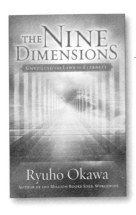

The Nine Dimensions

Unveiling the Laws of Eternity

Spirituality
Paperback · 5×8 · 176 pages
978-0-982698-56-3
US$15.95

In this book, Ryuho Okawa reveals that our souls were made to pursue spiritual evolution. He shows us that God designed this world and the vast, wondrous world of our afterlife as a school with many levels through which our souls learn and grow. We children of God have the potential for infinite growth as we strive to grow closer to His likeness. In addition to the joys we derive from our individual progress, God also gave humankind the objective of producing harmony and beauty from the diversity of our collective existence. This book is a window into the mind of our loving God, who encourages us to grow into greater angels. When the religions and cultures of the world discover the truth of their common spiritual origin, they will be inspired to accept their differences, come together under faith in God, and build an era of harmony and peaceful progress on Earth.

"What is God? God is light, and a part of
this light resides inside you."

The Moment of Truth

Become A Living Angel Today

Spirituality
Paperback · 5.2×7.3 · 160 pages
978-0-982698-57-0
US$14.95

The Moment of Truth: Become a Living Angel Today awakens
your soul to a hidden memory about your true roots as a child
of God. A part of God resides within you. This divine essence
provides you with the power to find your own salvation, even
amid adversities. Today, people have forgotten an essential truth:
that we all have the potential to work as God's angels, even as
we live on Earth. Okawa shows that we are essentially spiritual
beings and that our true and lasting happiness is not found within
the material world but rather in acts of unconditional and selfless
love toward the greater world.

These pages reveal God's mind, His mercy, and His hope that
many of us will become living angels that shine light onto this
world. Seek the light within yourself, and there you will find God's
Will, compassion, and dream to dispel darkness and conflict and
issue forth an era of worldwide peace on Earth.

Did you know that miracles are happening around us all the time?

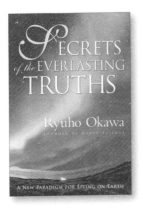

Secrets of the Everlasting Truths

A Spiritual Guide to Living Now

Spirituality
Paperback · 5.2×7.3 · 144 pages
978-1-937673-10-9
US$14.95

In this book, Ryuho Okawa shows us an extraordinary array of miracles that are increasing by the day. He reveals the fascinating truth that miracles occur through the help of Heaven and even space-people—with whom we Earth-people have shared a very close relationship for millennia. Through this book, Okawa shows us a glimpse of the power within knowing the existence of a vaster universe created by God. We are also on the brink of discovering the deeper truths about space-people and their influences on Earth. Indeed, our entire planet will experience a decisive paradigm shift of "knowledge" and "truth" which will lead to a new era of a paradoxical spirituality—in the future, the most scientific and physical of sciences, will require spiritual knowledge! The solutions to our current problems today are within our own minds.

For a complete list of books, visit OkawaBooks.com.